THE FINAL HARVEST

Medjugorje at the End of the Century

WAYNE WEIBLE

PARACLETE PRESS
Brewster, Massachusetts

Library of Congress Cataloging-in-Publication Data

Weible, Wayne.
    The final harvest : Medjugorje at the end of the century / by Wayne Weible
        p.   cm.
    Includes bibliographical references and index.
    ISBN 1-55725-223-8 (pbk.)
    1. Mary, Blessed Virgin, Saint—Apparitions and miracles—Bosnia and Hercegovina—Medugorje. 2. Medugorje (Bosnia and Hercegovina)—Church history—20th century. I. Title.
BT660.M44W43   1999
232.91'7'0949742—dc21   99-21287
                                                    CIP

10 9 8 7 6 5 4 3

Published by Paraclete Press
Brewster, Massachusetts
www.paraclete-press.com

Printed in the United States of America.

This book is dedicated to
the people of all faiths
who hear the messages of
the Blessed Virgin Mary at Medjugorje
and daily attempt to live them.

Table of Contents

3
Fruits

4
Storm

5
Harvest

ACKNOWLEDGMENTS

The messages reportedly given in apparition by the Blessed Virgin Mary at Medjugorje have been obtained and verified from a wide variety of qualified sources, the most important being personal contacts and interviews with the visionaries, priests, and others involved with the apparitions. All of the messages come under strict theological scrutiny by the priests in charge of the parish of Saint James Catholic Church, to assure they are in total compliance with Scripture and the doctrines of the Catholic Church.

If any message, event, or activity of the apparitions were not in conformity with this time-tested formula, the Church would condemn the phenomena immediately. After 18 years, no condemnation has occurred.

The wording and grammar of the messages are subject to the variance of translation from the Croatian language into English. No attempt is made to correct grammatically or change any part of the messages in order to retain their original flavor. Virtually all are given in the full text as they were received.

My thanks to family (especially my wife, Terri), friends, and fellow converts whose efforts contributed to the book, with a special thank-you to Terry and Cyril for their extraordinary efforts in gathering and verifying many of the early messages. Also, special thanks to my editor David Manuel, who always seems to bring out far more than I originally intend in my writing, and to Harriet Kunkle for her scrupulous editing of all the little details of writing.

I acknowledge that the final determination about the authenticity of a miraculous event occurring in Medjugorje rests with the investigation by the Catholic Church, and I submit entirely to its conclusion. However, based on thorough investigations by theological, scientific, and medical experts, and the consistently good spiritual fruits produced in the lives of many who have been touched by the message proclaimed by the Medjugorje visionaries, I accept the apparitions as authentic until final judgment is rendered. They are addressed as such in this book.

The Most Important Event of Our Time

A perceived supernatural religious phenomenon has become a reality for millions throughout the world. I am one of the millions. To those of us who believe in this phenomenon, it is the singular most important event of our times.

For more than 18 years, the Virgin Mary has appeared daily in apparition at the quiet, rural village of Medjugorje in Bosnia-Hercegovina. This unprecedented series of apparitions to six youths, and later by inner locution to two more young girls, began in June 1981. It continues to the date of this writing, with one overriding objective: to bring the world back to God. The apparitions are elevated in drama and urgency as the Blessed Virgin reveals that these will be her final apparitions on earth, because, as she adds, *"It will no longer be necessary. . . ."*

In the history of the Roman Catholic Church, the Virgin has appeared in apparition in many places throughout the ages, the most recognizable names of which are Guadalupe

(Mexico), La Salette and Lourdes (France), Knock (Ireland), and Fatima (Portugal). But never in recorded history has she appeared daily for so long a period of time, to so many chosen visionaries, with such profound global results.

The purpose is made clear in her messages. As a good mother, the Virgin Mary issues an urgent, repeated call for the children of the world to turn to God for true peace and happiness. That specific call was initiated in her apparitions in La Salette in 1846, was heightened at Fatima, and continues in Medjugorje. In this long-running, unconditional act of merciful heavenly love, it is the consistency of the call and the overwhelming response to it by so many people that leads to the belief that this is a final harvest of souls.

In Medjugorje, the Virgin gives powerful warnings of the consequences for a world continuing on the present path of godlessness. Yet, she does so with motherly love, identifying herself in these apparitions as the Queen of Peace. She pleads for reconciliation among all people on all levels of society and faith through prayer, fasting, and penance. She constantly emphasizes that she is only the messenger sent by God, and that it is up to each individual to exercise the gift of free will that God gave to humanity, and to accept or reject the offer to be included in the harvest.

In the summer of 1981, the village of Medjugorje, the republic of Bosnia-Hercegovina, and the entire region comprising what was then the Federation of Yugoslavia clearly represented a microcosm of the world. For centuries, the region had been engulfed in war or near-war, the cause of which was fueled so often by ethnic or religious persecution. In this mountainous region of Eastern Europe, the largely Slavic population consisted of three distinct groups—Croatians, Serbians, and Muslims—who constantly declared their hatred for one another.

Throughout history, the region has known no peace. Each generation has suffered seemingly endless cycles of invasion, resistance, and liberation. In between outside conquests, the region's inhabitants have practiced war on each other. Hate-filled reciprocal atrocities were quelled following World War II only through forced unity as the Federation of Yugoslavia fell under the dictatorship of an atheistic, Marxist government.

With such a bloody regional history, when the miracle of the apparitions began in Medjugorje in 1981, the people as a whole did not heed the call to reconciliation. Croat could not live with Serb, and neither could abide the Muslim Slavs, the descendants of Christians who had converted to Islam during the four centuries of Turkish conquest and rule. Still, the Virgin continued to appear daily to the children. Even though bloody civil war began in 1991, people continued to come on spiritual pilgrimage.

The pilgrims came during the worst times of the active conflict, not just for personal reasons, but to bring desperately needed material aid to hapless victims. Many had gone to Medjugorje previously on pilgrimage. Now they returned, without regard to personal danger or death. They were convinced that the Virgin was asking this of them through her messages. Their response was powerful evidence of the good seed that falls into fertile soil and gives off a hundredfold.

Today, in the midst of uneasy peace, widows, orphans, and grieving parents join pilgrims from around the world in Medjugorje. They are those who have lost loved ones, homes, and lands in this new holocaust. They are the same Croatians, Muslims, and Serbians who now come out of desperation to pray for a peace that only God can give them. Despite the people's widespread rejection of the messages, and the atrocities of the war that ensued, as of this writing, the Virgin Mary still appears daily to three of the original six visionaries. The harvest of souls continues.

The visionaries and locutionists are now young adults. All but two are married and have become parents. As predicted in the messages, the nondescript village has become famous as a popular site of religious pilgrimage. An estimated 30 million people have come seeking spiritual nourishment from virtually every part of the world.

The Blessed Virgin appears to Catholic Christian youths at Medjugorje, and her messages often ask adherence to the sacraments of the Roman Catholic Church. However, she makes clear from the beginning that her messages are for people of all beliefs. Regionally, that description includes Catholics, Orthodox, Muslims—even Marxist atheists. She states that she is the heavenly messenger for all of her "children of the world." The confirmation of that fact comes in the large number of non-Catholics who have been transformed spiritually. Among them is the author of this book.

I became interested in the apparitions of Medjugorje in October 1985, because I felt it would make a good story for the weekly newspapers my wife and I owned in our community of Myrtle Beach, South Carolina. As a journalist, trained professionally to be a skeptic, and as a Protestant of nominal faith with a disdain for such "Catholic things," I didn't believe the story of the apparitions at Medjugorje. As I was watching a recently made videotape about the apparitions—part of my research for the story—I was stunned when I suddenly felt a strong message placed in my heart asking me to make the spreading of the messages my life's mission. There was no doubt in my mind that this same Virgin Mary was speaking directly to me. Within months, we sold our businesses and made the spreading of the Medjugorje message through writing and lecturing our full-time work.

Having authored three books on the apparitions, I have not made it my purpose here just to retell the story, nor necessarily to provide authenticated proof of the apparitions. My objective is to present the spiritual story and the impact of the Medjugorje phenomena, using as my main format a majority of the messages just as they were given to the visionaries. The messages require little explanation or commentary. I have begun with the first messages and included those given right up to the time of publication of this book.

Interspersed among the messages I have placed factual details, stories, and personal commentary gleaned from 14 years of involvement and investigation. This information lends witness by example far better than could be accomplished through reams of facts, theology, and debate. I have placed special emphasis on stories garnered from the war, which raged for nearly four years.

Without sounding a frantic or apocalyptic note, I have made it my major emphasis to show the direct impact of these particular apparitions on the world. I believe it is with deliberate purpose that the Virgin Mary has been sent to the world at this time to appear as never before in history. The final harvest of souls is a harvest of love and mercy, not of gloom and doom.

The Virgin has told us that at the conclusion of the apparitions, the world will undergo a spiritual cleansing that will mark the beginning of an unprecedented era of peace through a full return to God. Yet that cleansing is unequivocally not the end of the physical world.

Last, I have undertaken to give a general update as the apparitions continue into an unprecedented nineteenth year of daily occurrence. This update includes the present status of the visionaries, the villagers, and the visiting pilgrims, and focuses on the spiritual fruits of each.

It is these fruits, which have been discovered by people of all faiths—and no faith, that this book desires to reveal to the reader. Its singular objective is to renew spiritually and strengthen individuals reading about the apparitions at Medjugorje for the first time—as well as those already familiar with them. It is left to the readers of this book to decide how the message of Medjugorje will affect their lives.

My hope is that it will leave each one wanting to be among the souls of the final harvest.

—*Wayne Weible*

PART I

Seeds

I want you to know, brethren, that I have often intended to come to you . . . in order that I may reap some harvest among you as well as among the rest of the Gentiles. I am under obligation both to Greeks and to barbarians, both to the wise and to the foolish. . . .

—ROMANS 1:13–14.

1

The Message

The young Franciscan priest from Bosnia-Hercegovina stared blankly out the window as the plane approached the airport. It was the first week of May 1981, and the weather was nearly perfect. Normally, this would be a time of joy and anticipation as he prepared to attend an important international leader's conference of the Catholic Charismatic Renewal in Rome, Italy. At the moment, he only hoped the conference would rekindle the Holy Spirit flame within him that had strongly marked his brief priesthood.

The apathy of the people in his parish and surrounding parishes had brought Father Tomislav Vlasic to this discouraging point. He had come to his assignment at Saint Francis of Assisi Catholic Church in Capljina, filled with a fervor expressed well through a strong gift of preaching and a magnetic personality. As a result, the young priest had been invited to nearby villages to preach the message of the Gospels. But instead of spiritual conversion, he was met with indifference. Many young people did not attend Mass; work on Sundays was the norm. Families praying the rosary together seemed to be a thing of the past.

Tomislav came to the conference with one thought in mind: to seek help through the wisdom of two well-known members of the Charismatic Movement, Sister Briege McKenna and Father Emiliano Tardif. Both would be speakers at the conference. He wanted them to pray over him in hopes of discerning the answer to restoring his spiritual buoyancy and overcoming the resistance of the people at home.

Father Tomislav's prayers were answered, but in a way that far exceeded his expectations. Sister Briege McKenna, an Irish nun living in the United States, had a powerful healing ministry and a strong gift of prophecy. As she prayed over Father Tomislav, she began describing a vivid prophetic vision, telling him that she "saw him in a twin-towered church sitting in a chair and surrounded by a great crowd." There were streams of water flowing from beneath the chair out onto the people, she related, "streams of powerful healing water. . . ."

Tomislav was deeply touched by the vision, but also confused. The only church he knew with twin towers was twelve miles away in the parish of Medjugorje. But he was happy, having received far more than he had anticipated through the encounter with Sister Briege. Surely, this was a sign that the people were finally going to respond to his ministry. What occurred next raised his spirits well above mere happiness, even though the young priest was not quite certain what it meant.

Also gifted with the charisma of a healing ministry, Father Emiliano Tardif, a French-Canadian presently stationed in Colombia, South America, came to Tomislav the following day. He also had prayed over him. Taking him aside and embracing him, he said, "My dear young friend, I have a wonderful message for you from Jesus. He says, 'Don't worry, I am sending you my mother!'"

And a great portent appeared in heaven, a woman clothed with the sun, with the moon under her feet, and on her head a crown of twelve stars. . . .
—REVELATION 12:1.

2

Preparing the Way

The old woman groaned as she straightened from a long period of bending over to prune the young tobacco plants. She wiped her brow and glanced down the row of plants where an equally aged companion doing the same task worked her way towards her. It was mid-morning in early May 1981, yet another hard day of work in one of the tobacco fields that dotted the landscape of the tiny village of Medjugorje. Their weathered faces bore evidence of years of such labor.

The monotony and stress of the hard work was offset by their constant praying of the rosary in a steady, low-pitched monotone as they worked toward each other. This mixing of labor and devout prayer was a way of life among the older women of the village, and it had been so for generations.

Suddenly, the woman stopped still and stared. She shook her head, rubbed her eyes and looked again. There, in a clear vision out of a flash of light, floating eerily in her direction above the row of tobacco plants, was what appeared to be an ancient chariot drawn by two white horses. It moved steadily but silently, slowly passing over her. As it did, she saw that the chariot contained a very old man with long white hair and a long white beard. The vision then slowly faded, as the woman, sensing something spiritual in the mysterious phenomenon, acknowledged what her eyes had seen by reverently making the sign of the cross. She then numbly returned to her work.

When she met her companion in the middle of the row, they paused and looked at each other. Hesitatingly, the woman gestured in the direction where the vision had faded away and asked, "Did you see—?"

"Yes," her companion answered in a whisper, nodding slowly, "yes, I saw it."

After an extended silence, each again made the sign of the cross and resumed working the tobacco plants.

Several weeks later, in the parish of Medjugorje with its twin-towered Saint James Church, a beautiful young woman, identifying herself as the Blessed Virgin Mary, made her first appearance on a hillside to six Croatian youths. This was the first of what would become daily supernatural apparitions that would take the village, the region, and eventually the entire world to unprecedented spiritual heights—well past the wildest dreams of Father Tomislav.

The date of this first apparition was clearly no mere coincidence: The most dazzling and powerful apparitions of the Virgin Mary in history began on the twenty-fourth day of June, recognized in the Roman Catholic Church as the Feast Day of Saint John, the Baptist.

And as they still went on and talked, behold, a chariot of fire
and horses of fire separated the two of them. And Elijah
went up by a whirlwind into heaven. —2 KINGS 2:11–12.

And the disciples asked him, "Then why do the scribes say that
first Elijah must come?" He replied, "Elijah does come, and he is to
restore all things; but I tell you that Elijah has already come, and
they did not know him, but did to him whatever they pleased. So also
the Son of man will suffer at their hands." Then the disciples
understood that he was speaking to them of John the Baptist.
—MATTHEW 17:10–13.

3

Seeds of a Miracle

The figure of a young woman in a shimmering brilliance of light smiled at the six youths kneeling before her. She then slowly raised her arms, smiled, and softly said to them: *Praise be Jesus!* The date was June 25, 1981.

At the time of this writing, some 18 years later, the apparitions of the Virgin Mary at the little village of Medjugorje continue daily. Each encounter begins with this same phrase, which serves as confirmation that the apparitions are indeed an ongoing gift of grace from heaven, a grace that has spread steadily throughout the world.

The apparitions had actually begun the previous evening, June 24, 1981, as a startled teenager, 15-year-old Ivanka Ivankovic, was the first to see the vision. The young girl was soon joined by several of her peers. The figure, bathed in an unearthly light and hovering about 50 yards up the side of a small hill near the village, smiled continuously and held an infant in her arms as she beckoned to the children to come to her. From a strong Catholic upbringing, the children immediately recognized her as the Virgin Mary.

But they were too frightened to respond, frozen in place by fear, some praying, and some weeping. One of the boys, Ivan Dragicevic, 16, took one look and ran away. As a light mist of rain began to fall, the others slowly backed away from the scene, then turned and ran swiftly to their homes, where they excitedly told family and friends what had happened. News spread through the small community like wild fire: "Gospa"[1] had appeared in their village!

The following evening, June 25, each of the youths who had seen the vision the previous day felt an irresistible inner urge to return to the scene. Again, the figure appeared, this time without the infant in her arms whom she would later identify as the baby Jesus. When she beckoned to the children, they raced up the side of the bramble-covered, rocky slopes at a speed normally beyond their physical ability. It was a climb that usually took 12 to 15 minutes, but they did it in only two. Kneeling less than five feet away, Ivanka and Ivan were joined by Mirjana Dragicevic, 15, Marija Pavlovic, 16, Vicka Ivankovic, 17, and Jakov Colo, only ten.

Within minutes, fear gave way to youthful curiosity and questions poured forth: Who are you? Why have you come? What do you want? The figure in the light, after identifying herself as the Blessed Virgin Mary, told them, *I have come to tell you that God exists and that He loves you. I have come because there are many true believers here. I wish to be with you to convert and to reconcile the whole world.*

The children stared in awe. Mirjana, who with Ivanka was the first to see the Blessed Virgin, then asked, "Why are you appearing to us? We are no better than others." The Virgin smiled and paused before answering, *I do not necessarily choose the best* (people).

This was a telling response. On the previous evening, Ivanka and Mirjana, having finished evening chores, had slipped off to a secluded spot to listen to rock music while smoking cigarettes pilfered from their fathers. To millions who would later journey to Medjugorje on pilgrimage, this venial act of experimentation would serve as an example that God chooses ordinary people for extraordinary missions. Those chosen for a charisma that allows them to see a heavenly visitor are chosen not necessarily because of the good they may have done, but for the good they can do.

This first apparition with conversation lasted for what seemed a long time to the children; they didn't want it to end, but they were too awed to ask more questions. One of them finally asked, "Will you come back?" *Yes,* the Virgin responded, *to the same place as yesterday.*

The entire scene just described was witnessed by a small crowd of local villagers who had come to the site on this second day, as word had spread quickly that the children were claiming to have seen the Virgin Mary on the hill. Few had believed them, including family members. Vicka's sister had asked playfully if maybe she had seen a flying saucer, while Marija had laughed at first when an uncle had teased her sister Milka, who had briefly seen the Virgin with Ivanka and Mirjana on the first day.

Now, on this second day, Marija was there in place of her sister, who, much to her distress, was made to tend to the family sheep. Marija had come along with little Jakov, who had been visiting at her home at the time that Ivanka had come to her door in search of Milka, excitedly shouting that the Virgin was appearing again.

By the third day—Friday, June 26—the entire region was

abuzz with excitement over the reported apparitions. As the six youths knelt again in a state of ecstasy, a crowd estimated at nearly three thousand reacted in emotion-driven confusion. Vicka's grandmother had told her to take holy water to sprinkle on the vision if she appeared again. An age-old tradition for the villagers, sprinkling holy water was a test to make sure this apparent miracle was from God. When the vision made her appearance, Vicka threw the entire contents of the bottle on the figure, and said, "If you are not from God, go away!" In response, the figure smiled a radiant smile, pleased with the test.

What happened next would set the stage for the Virgin's major purpose of coming in apparition to this specific site. As the apparition ended, the visionaries were separated from each other as villagers tugged at them and begged for details of their encounter. Marija, finding herself alone, made her way down the pathway of Podbrdo Hill.

All at once, she felt a mysterious tug that moved her to the side of the trail, where suddenly the Virgin appeared to her again. The radiant happiness of the beautiful young woman in the light was now transformed into somber concern. She stood in front of the image of an empty, rainbow-colored cross, tears pouring down her cheeks as she pleaded, *Peace, Peace, Peace! Be reconciled! Only Peace! Make your peace with God among yourselves. For that, it is necessary to believe, to pray, to fast, and to go to confession.*

These words were an impassioned warning that would be repeated over and over again in the succeeding days, months, and years. The Virgin Mary had indeed come with a message of reassurance that God was real, a message of peace and love. But it was also a warning, to the world as a whole, but also to the three ethnic groups that formed the population of Yugoslavia. The world was ablaze with nationalist poison as even the smallest ethnic group fought fiercely for recognition and independence. Historically, the result of such ethnic chauvinism had been the bloodshed of many innocent people, coupled with a vicious struggle for control driven by the twin motivators of power and greed.

As the Virgin appeared on the hill that first evening, holding the infant Jesus in her arms, it was as if she were renewing the birth of the Son of God in a village that very much resembled Bethlehem. In her messages she would emphasize that she came seeking the only true peace there is—for the world, and specifically for the people of that region.

Even with the impact of such a miracle, the people, including the religious leaders of the three ethnic groups, would largely ignore her warning call for reconciliation. The tantalizing lure of immediate prestige and power overwhelmed the bleak promise of long-suffering peace. Ten years later, a devastating, horror-filled war would result, leaving the countries comprising former Yugoslavia free from the bonds of Communism, but in shambles. The deaf ear turned toward the Blessed Virgin's call for peace would be yet another of the world's countless rejections of heaven's promise of true peace through the birth, crucifixion, and resurrection of Jesus Christ.

But for the immediate time, the awesome reality of the apparitions created for the masses an emotional atmosphere of repentance, conversion, and unlimited hope.

Surprising the visionaries and the church hierarchy, the apparitions continued daily. As the young visionaries received startling messages, the crowds from the surrounding area continued to grow in size. Then came an astonishing revelation.

Just a month before the apparitions began, Ivanka's

mother had died suddenly. She had been rushed to the hospital in the nearby city of Mostar with a serious illness, but no one expected her death. Her daughter Ivanka was left lonely and depressed. Now the young girl was on the hill overlooking her home, able to see and converse with a beautiful lady who claimed to be from heaven. Her question was inevitable: "Dear Lady, where is my mother?" The answer filled the young girl with unbounded joy: *Your mother is in heaven with us!*

This astounding news reverberated through the village and surrounding communities. People wanted to know why this woman had gone straight to heaven, since she had done nothing particularly special in life. But she had been a good mother and wife and had lived her faith daily with prayers and frequent attendance at Mass, accepting what God had given her in life and fulfilling the responsibility that came with it. The ensuing messages would emphasize this basic requirement for holiness.

By now, however reluctant, the local church was becoming involved. The initial reaction to the youths' claims of seeing the Madonna daily, ranged from total rejection to calls for exorcism. Cautious and even skeptical Franciscan priests urged the visionaries to request a sign from the Virgin to prove that the apparitions were really from God. Her response was calm and direct: *Blessed are those who have not seen and who believe.*

Many priests remained skeptical. The young visionaries were questioned sharply in long sessions with the Franciscans. Worse was the interrogation by the local Communist authorities, who accused the children of using drugs, or of being mentally disturbed, or of just plain lying. Others said it was a prank that had gotten out of hand, or a deliberate hoax perpetrated by the Franciscans themselves.

Through this ordeal, the six youths remained steadfast. They had seen and were continuing to see the Virgin each evening, they stated repeatedly in the face of the questioning by all camps. No threats against them or their families could sway them from this claim.

Within weeks, thousands were coming to the village for the daily apparition. A pattern was soon established: Following a period of prayer led by the visionaries, the Virgin would appear to them after three sudden bursts of a brilliant light that was sometimes visible to a few in the crowd. The children would then fall to their knees in synchronization after stopping their prayers on the exact same word, sometimes even on the same syllable, staring at the spot where she was apparently appearing. Each would seemingly be in conversation with her, separate from the others, his or her mouth moving to form words, but without making any sound audible to the onlookers.

The apparition, occurring always close to the same time each evening, would last for periods of time ranging from a few minutes to an hour. It depended, the visionaries explained, on the needs presented and the teachings of the Virgin during the time of the apparition. Afterwards, the visionaries would describe their experience to the people, even telling them what the Virgin looked like.

The children saw the Virgin Mary in a three-dimensional way, just as we see each other, they would explain: She was very Croatian in appearance, about 19–21 years of age, approximately 5 feet 7 inches tall, slender in form, and indescribably beautiful beyond any statue or picture they had seen. She had blue eyes, a pale ivory-white complexion, and a small curl of black hair showing on the left side of her face from under a long white veil that reached down in length to a small white cloud that covered her feet. The cloud, the children stated, grew with the length of time the Virgin remained in apparition. Her dress was described as being long and without a sash, and of a lucent, silver-gray color. And, they added, she had a crown of twelve stars circling her head.

Podbrdo Hill, once a secluded pasture for the sheep of the villagers, was now covered daily with people. Relatives brought the sick and the handicapped, begging the visionaries to ask Gospa's intercession for a healing. The parents of one handicapped child asked the visionaries to intercede on behalf of their son. The little boy could not hear or speak, and he walked with a limp. The question was put to the Virgin, and after looking at the little boy and his family for a long time, she gave her reply: *Have them believe strongly in his cure. Go in the peace of God.*

The child's parents were disappointed in the answer: They had expected immediate healing for their son. The Virgin Mary was telling them to pray, have faith, and trust. But they obeyed.

Later that evening, as they made their way home, the family stopped at a small restaurant. Suddenly, the little boy grabbed a cup and banged it on the table and said, "Momma, I want milk!" Within a short period of time, he could hear and speak, and soon was running and playing with other boys.

As news of the healing spread, questions and requests for healing grew daily. The Virgin responded in a very human way one day when, with a smile, she raised her hands, turned her eyes to heaven and exclaimed, *God, help us all!*

In July, there was a startling addition to the apparitions. In answer to repeated pleas from the youths about how they would be able to continue as visionaries, they were shown

Jesus' head in a vision, and were able to see clearly His brown eyes, beard, and long hair. This vision of Jesus was given to them, they were told, to prepare them for the suffering and persecution they were to endure as visionaries. Mary then told them, *My angels, I send you my Son, Jesus, who was tortured for His faith, and yet He endured everything. You also, my angels, will endure everything.*

She implored them to pray and have faith that they would survive this initial harassment and skepticism. How must we pray, they asked? *Continue to recite the Lord's Prayer, the Hail Mary, and the Glory Be* (in sequence) *seven times, but also add the Creed. Good-bye, my angels, go in the peace of God.*

Using this traditional prayer of the grandmothers of the region, the Virgin introduced the first lesson in prayer to her young seers. Later, she would ask for the rosary to be prayed daily—not just by Catholics, but by all people. Prayer, especially the rosary, would become the mainstay of all her messages.

It was soon evident that the lives of all involved would never be the same. These early events would be but the beginning of the final harvest of souls.

And he told them many things in parables, saying: "A sower went out to sow. And as he sowed, some seeds fell along the path, and the birds came and devoured them. Other seeds fell on rocky ground, where they had not much soil, and immediately they sprang up, since they had no depth of soil, but when the sun rose they were scorched; and since they had no root they withered away. Other seeds fell upon thorns, and the thorns grew up and choked them. Other seeds fell on good soil and brought forth grain, some a hundredfold, some sixty, some thirty. He who has ears, let him hear."

—MATTHEW 13:3–9.

4
Good Soil

Medjugorje had the potential to someday be good soil for spiritual conversion. Throughout the centuries of turmoil and struggle, the villagers had clung stubbornly to their Catholic faith. In 1933, as a visible sign of that faith, they had constructed a huge concrete cross atop the mountain overlooking their fertile valley. Their official reason for doing so had been to honor 1,900 years of the cross. Privately, they might have admitted to erecting the cross out of a mixture of faith and spiritual superstition, to gain protection for their crops, the virtual life-blood of the people.

With the ongoing daily apparitions taking place, questions arose: "Was the cross constructed as part of heaven's plan to bring renewal of God to the people of the world through the apparitions?" Or, "Was this field for spiritual harvest chosen because of the act of faith by its people?" For the believer, either question could be answered in the affirmative.

For the skeptics, more obvious questions remained.

Among them were these: "Why would heaven choose such an unlikely place to reveal astounding supernatural messages to the world?" And, "Why would such an awesome responsibility be placed in the hands of peasant children?" Again, for the believer the answers were clear.

Medjugorje is small, rural, and indistinguishable from hundreds of villages scattered throughout the mountainous region of which it is a part—that is, except for the cross atop the small mountain overlooking their valley. The 15-ton, 36-foot-high concrete monolith reflects accurately the character and faith of the villagers. Legend has it that an actual relic of the original cross is embedded in its base. Years of harsh weather have aged and discolored the cross, and have chipped away chunks of cement from its edges. But its beauty and effect go beyond the exterior. The same can be said for the village and its people.

Most of western Hercegovina is poor and undeveloped, with little industry. The soil of the Brotnjo region, of which Medjugorje is a part, is hard and stony. But once cleared, it is excellent, arable land for crop growing. After extremely hard manual labor, it becomes good soil, providing high quality tobacco, splendid fruit trees, and fine vineyards that produce superior wines. Through years of working the land, the residents of the region have become hardy, resilient, and self-sufficient.

For the people living in Medjugorje in June 1981, resiliency was a must. It was also the root of a strong adherence to their Catholic faith. Under a Serb-dominated Marxist government, the practice of religion was grudgingly allowed, but atheism was taught formally in the schools, and children of religious families were ridiculed. Only those loyal to the Communist party line could hold important public jobs. Except for the most menial positions, most believers therefore depended for their livelihood on the land and on a few farm animals.

The young visionaries were representative of the villagers. Life for them was filled with daily chores and school. They were neither overly pious nor terribly bad. They were, as Mirjana herself would later describe, "neither good or bad, just like everyone else." She went on to say, "When the apparitions began, my grandmother said: 'Why should Gospa appear to the likes of you when you go around with boys?' I told her, well, she knows what we're like, and she doesn't want us to pretend to be something we're not!"

Yet, while ordinary in the sense of being part of the village, the children chosen to be visionaries were very different from each other in temperament and personality. Prior to the apparitions, only three of them were close friends. Vicka, Ivanka, and Mirjana were nearly inseparable, and while they were acquainted with the others, they had little in common with them other than school and the close proximity of their homes. Their initial coming together as visionaries confused and frightened them. During the harsh harassment and stress of the first days, there was a mini-struggle for leadership, with Mirjana and Vicka dominating. In a period of just a few days however, under the guidance of the Blessed Virgin they developed into a close-knit unit, with each having a distinct but informal role.

Mirjana was actually an outsider who, although having been born in Medjugorje, now lived and attended school in Sarajevo, coming to Medjugorje in the summers to stay with her grandparents. Bright and articulate, she was very much the typical teenager, her head filled with things of the world. By her own admission, she had paid little attention to spirituality, and she attended church more out of habit than desire. Personal prayer was rare for Mirjana. Hoping for a career in agronomy, she was attending the university in Sarajevo.

Pretty, blonde, and outgoing, Mirjana became a natural leader and spokesperson for the visionaries. At times, some thought she went too far, adding personal interpretations to parts of the messages. She was also the main target for accusations. Because she had come from the city, rumors began that she might have brought drugs to the village and convinced the others to try them, creating a hallucinatory effect of having seen this mysterious figure in the light. Such rumors died in the following days due to the consistency of the visionaries' stories.

Mirjana's good friend Ivanka, the first to see the Virgin, was amazed to be included as a visionary. She, too, was typical in her teenage ways. A very attractive, dark-haired girl, Ivanka was sure of her path in life. She intended to marry as quickly as possible and settle in the village to raise her family as part of a lifestyle that had changed little over the centuries.

But Ivanka had just lost her mother, and she was in a state of grief and depression at the time the apparitions began. Naturally, skeptics assumed that since she was the first to see the apparition, she was trying desperately to replace the loss of her mother by claiming to see the Virgin. That theory might have had credibility if the apparitions had lasted only a few days, but with the passing weeks, her story did not change. Ivanka's grief was replaced with strenuous responsibility and ongoing harassment as she continued her claim of seeing the apparition. Her joy came in the moments of the apparitions; these daily encounters were more than enough to sustain her.

Marija, quiet and good-natured, gained the role as one of the six visionaries that possibly had been meant for her 13-year-old sister Milka, who along with Ivan, Mirjana, Vicka, and Ivanka had seen the vision on the first day. When these four came running to Milka's home the following day, claiming that the apparition was occurring again, Milka was working in the fields on orders from her mother, who did not believe her daughter's claim of having seen the apparition. Instead of Milka, the four youths found Marija and little Jakov, who was visiting Marija. Marija and Jacov accompanied the others to the hill in Milka's place, thus completing the contingent of six youths who would become daily visionaries.

After Marija had experienced the apparition on the second day, her mother was convinced that Milka had truly seen the Virgin Mary on the first day as she had claimed. Marija insisted that her sister accompany her the next day and stand right behind her. Milka did, but sadly, she was unable to see the vision. And so the number of visionaries remained six.

Marija was gifted with an ability to make everyone around her comfortable and at ease. Unobtrusive and humble, she had planned to become a beautician. But after several weeks of the apparitions, she stated she wanted to enter a convent, adding that before the apparitions, God had been distant; now, she wanted to give the rest of her life to serving Him.

Cheerful, outgoing and possessing a radiant, seemingly perpetual smile, Vicka easily became the "ambassador" of the apparitions. Prior to that fateful day of the first apparition, Vicka's family was known for having a strong faith. One priest stated with some amusement that most evenings the neighbors could hear Vicka's family loudly reciting prayers. Another priest who had taught Vicka her catechism, described her as incapable of telling a lie.

This vibrant young girl seemed to have no fear of authority, answering priest and pilgrim alike when asked mundane questions about the apparitions. On one occasion, a priest asked Vicka about a particular message; after she had given her answer, the priest asked, "Are you sure?" Vicka laughed and said, "Of course I'm sure, I was there!" On another occasion, local authorities took the children to police headquarters for questioning; there, a policeman threatened Vicka, putting a gun to her temple in an attempt to intimidate her. Testily, she gave a short laugh and said, "Why would you waste a bullet on the likes of me when the economy is so bad?"

Ivan was almost the direct opposite of Vicka. Shy, serious, and introverted, he was visibly uncomfortable around pilgrims and the media and did not enjoy the notoriety of being a visionary. But he was in a constant state of awe that the Virgin Mary had chosen him. He later explained that when he first saw the apparition on the hillside, he ran away out of fear that he had never really acknowledged God as a part of his life. Ivan immediately went to his room, locked the door, and began to pray. His mother was stunned, and would later state that she believed her son was actually seeing the Virgin when she found a rosary in his pants pocket as she was doing the laundry.

Two months later, Ivan would enter a seminary with the intention of becoming a priest, an attempt that would fail both academically and personally. But Ivan's desire and effort indicated just how deeply he was spiritually moved by the realization that the Blessed Virgin Mary was appearing daily to him and the others at Medjugorje.

The question on the minds of many villagers was why ten-year-old Jakov had been included doing among the selected visionaries. A clever, impish, strong-headed boy, he was very much like other young boys his age, and quite unlikely to be an integral part of such a miracle. His interests lay far from prayer and church attendance; much more to his liking were sports, especially soccer. Even after his inclusion as a visionary, he was not above once asking the Virgin to tell him the score of an upcoming championship soccer match that included one of his favorite teams! She merely smiled.

Jakov's father was rarely present in their small hovel of a home. To support his family, the father was constantly away working as a migrant worker in Austria, leaving the task of raising his only son to his wife. Thus, the little boy immersed himself in games as an escape from the harsh realities of daily life. But once the visions became a regular part of each day, Jakov was always in attendance at the evening Mass. He spoke with awe about the Virgin; her daily appearance became the most important part of his life, and he spoke with seriousness and pointed politeness when interviewed by media and priests.

These were the young people elevated to instant notoriety as visionaries of a unique supernatural religious phenomenon that would transform them and their village forever. The transformation would be spiritual, but the individual personalities would remain the same, as would the character of the village. Medjugorje had become new holy ground. Yet, for the children and the village, the basic essence of what had always been, remained.

As the Virgin continued to appear, the visionaries quickly developed into not just conveyers of her messages but examples of them as well. Each assumed a specific role, with greater responsibility given in the early months to Mirjana, Vicka, and Marija.

Mirjana seemed to have received a deeper understanding

about the state of the church. Her good friend Vicka became the dominant mystic, with the responsibility to reveal the fate of the world as given through the messages. Marija was chosen to give particular messages to pilgrims and priests; later, she would be the one to receive and communicate the messages meant for the general public. Each was also given responsibility to pray for specific intentions: Mirjana for unbelievers, Vicka and Jakov for the sick and handicapped, Marija for souls in purgatory, Ivan for youth, and Ivanka for families.

Medjugorje, a humble place, a place of little things and unchanging daily life, a place not even found on most maps, had seemingly become a new Bethlehem through these supernatural apparitions. Six young people, ordinary in every sense by outward appearances, had become relaters of heavenly messages meant for the entire world. It all seemed so unlikely. Yet, God's ways are ageless: He chooses poverty, simplicity, littleness, and the ordinary in order to manifest Himself.

The skeptics and unbelievers still scoffed. But for those who had eyes to see, the answers to the questions about why this place and these children were chosen, were clear; the fruits of transformation were abundant. People began to change as a deep, spiritual peace settled over the village.

At that time Jesus declared, "I thank thee, Father, Lord of heaven and earth, that thou hast hidden these things from the wise and understanding and revealed them to babes." —MATTHEW 11:25.

5
The Planting

Much to the surprise of the visionaries and the entire village, the apparitions continued into September 1981. Having no previous knowledge of past apparitions, the visionaries were told about Lourdes, France, where the Blessed Virgin had appeared a total of 18 times. Thus, they assumed that she would appear at Medjugorje the same number of times. Once the eighteenth daily apparition had come and gone, they asked her how much longer she was going to appear. In answer, she smiled, paused, and then said: *Is it, after all that I am boring you?*

She later added, when asked the same question again, *As long as you wish, my angels!* Was it possible, they wondered, that she would continue coming every day? The news spread rapidly throughout the region and soon even larger crowds were coming to Medjugorje. The influx of visitors created heavy overloads on utilities, pushing reserves to the maximum. Daily work was disrupted; roads were jammed, creating rare traffic snarls. And the Franciscan priests of the parish were unsure just what to do with so many people seeking spiritual guidance and answers to questions about the apparitions.

The local Communist authorities were fearful that an insurrection was about to take place. They continued mercilessly to harass the visionaries, threatening them and members of their families. Without notice, they would pick them up and transport them to police headquarters in nearby Citluk for long hours of questioning. Family members were threatened with the loss of their jobs and arrest if the "nonsense" did not cease. Pilgrims coming to the area were stopped, searched, and delayed for hours.

The harshest threats were saved for Franciscan priest Jozo Zovko, pastor of Saint James Church—by this time a strong supporter and spiritual director for the children, and for the bishop of the diocese, Pavao Zanic. Government officials made it clear to them both that they wanted the daily gatherings stopped immediately. The blunt alternative was jail.

In the beginning, Father Jozo, who had been pastor in Medjugorje for only six months prior to the start of the apparitions, severely questioned the children. He could not understand why people were not coming to the church for Mass and confession if these visions were really from God. Several weeks after they had begun, the villagers were still flocking to the hill every evening. He sat alone in his church one evening in deep prayer, asking God for a sign if this was indeed from Him. Suddenly he heard distinctly a male voice say, *First, go out and protect the children.*

Startled, Father Jozo looked around the church. The message was repeated. The sound of banging on the church door interrupted his encounter, and when he opened the door, all six of the young visionaries came tumbling in, pleading for him to protect them as the police were chasing them. The pastor quickly whisked them to the rectory and placed them in a small room before returning to the front of the building, determined to protect them. Within minutes the police came and brusquely asked Father Jozo if he had seen the children. He told them he had, but, surprisingly, they did not wait to hear more and ran off in another direction.

Father Jozo and the children returned to the church. A short time later, the Virgin appeared in apparition and the priest who had doubted was suddenly able to see her just as the children did. From that moment, he became their staunchest supporter and defender, a role that would soon cost him his freedom.

In October, the authorities made good on their threat. Father Jozo was arrested and charged with fostering insurrection through a highly charged sermon he delivered shortly after he himself witnessed the Virgin in apparition. The civil authorities deemed the homily as a direct attack on the Marxist system of government. This was just the excuse they needed to arrest the priest, and thus, they hoped, bring the apparitions to an end. Father Jozo was convicted and served 18 months of a three-year sentence.

By contrast, the church authorities took a kinder view of the apparitions at first. Bishop Zanic was so interested in the events at Medjugorje that in the beginning weeks, he made five visits to the parish to see and talk with the visionaries and the priests. In a homily in July 1981, the bishop proclaimed his belief for all the world to hear: "Six simple children like these would have told all in half an hour, if anybody had been manipulating them. I assure you that none of the priests have done any such thing . . . furthermore, I am convinced the children are not lying. . ."

What could have happened to cause the bishop to change his mind so radically? Simply put, it was fostered by the escalation of a petty squabble between Franciscan and secular priests,[2] one that elevated in proportion. The bishop was not a Franciscan and therein lay the problem. The Franciscans had been there for centuries serving the people through the worst times of invasion and war, so much so that they were referred to affectionately as "uncles" by the faithful.

In September 1980, the year before the apparitions began, the newly named Bishop of Mostar began shifting parishes in his diocese from Franciscan to secular authority. The Franciscans asked the bishop to reconsider this move, as did the people of the parishes in question. It was the parishioners who vigorously insisted that Franciscan priests assigned to the parishes in question continue to serve, which they did.

When Bishop Zanic learned of this, he retaliated by making an example of two of the most popular young Franciscans, initiating action to have them expelled from their order—and from the priesthood. Holy war broke out. It was a situation, which could have and should have been handled quietly within the diocese. But true to the heritage of the region, it became a crux of public confrontation and was dubbed unofficially the "Hercegovina Case."

Worsening the situation, the visionaries were persuaded by a Franciscan priest to ask the Blessed Virgin to comment on the problem. Surprisingly, she did. According to the visionaries, she stated that the bishop had been "misled and misinformed," and "should reconsider" his banning of the two Franciscans. That did it. When Bishop Zanic heard this message delivered to him in fervent terms personally by Vicka, he exclaimed, "The Blessed Mother of God would never speak to a bishop that way!"

From that moment on he became a staunch opponent of the apparitions.

The turn of events concerning the bishop was accompanied by a renewed call by the Virgin for the people to listen to her messages and begin acting on her requests for prayer, fasting, penance, and frequent confession. If heaven's plan through the apparitions was to succeed, the Church would have to be intricately involved; there was no other way. Matters were soon put back on the right track, ironically, by orders from the government to move the apparitions from the hillside. There were to be no more outside demonstrations; if the young people and the villagers insisted on continuing these gatherings, they must move them into the church.

Thus, the apparitions were soon occurring each evening in a small side chapel to the right of the altar of Saint James Church. Huge crowds now filled the church and its surrounding grounds. Under the direction of the priests, a daily spiritual regimen was soon implemented. These spiritual practices would become the foundation of conversion for millions throughout the world. Unbeknownst to the authorities, their harassment accomplished exactly what the Virgin desired of the people.

As envisioned by Sister Briege McKenna, when she had prayed over Father Tomislav Vlasic at the Rome Charismatic conference, the "living spiritual waters" were now flowing freely in Medjugorje. Father Tomislav was now the pastor at Saint James, taking the place of the imprisoned Father Jozo. Each afternoon, overflowing crowds would gather early to pray the rosary in preparation for the Virgin's appearance. Following the apparition, the faithful would complete the prayers begun earlier and then attend Mass. Afterwards, the people would pray the glorious mysteries of the rosary, and then close the evening with the prayers requested by the Virgin in the early days of the apparitions: the Creed, followed by seven Our Father's, seven Hail Mary's, and seven Glory Be's.

Even though many throughout the region paid little attention to the apparitions, the villagers themselves were changing. They were attending evening Mass regularly; few were working in the evenings or on Sundays. There were noticeable differences in how they treated each other as the family feuds that had been a trademark of the community began to fade.

These important changes had begun in the early weeks of the apparitions. Father Jozo, now convinced the apparitions were from God, knew that unless the people accepted the messages in thought, word and deed, the purpose of the supernatural grace would fail. The people of Medjugorje and the surrounding region had to become examples for those who would come in the future from around the world.

Shortly after undergoing his own transformation from skeptic to believer, Father Jozo called an evening meeting in the church. Once congregated, the villagers were shocked to hear the pastor of Saint James tell them of his own experience with seeing the Virgin. They must become the example; therefore, he concluded, no one was leaving the church until they forgave each other. He then folded his arms and waited.

There was uneasy shifting and a low, continuous murmur. Finally a burly villager stood up, red-faced and nervous. He walked over to another man with whom he had feuded for years, and stuck out his hand. The man stood up and instead of taking his hand, embraced him, a rare act between Croatian men so hardened by daily toil and years of oppression. In seconds, the church was a happy bedlam as mass forgiveness began the conversion process for the people of Medjugorje.

The new wave of spiritual conversion continued to grow. At each apparition, the visionaries asked questions, and the Virgin gave her reply. Now the people were anxiously awaiting each message. It was soon evident that every message and answer was simply a confirmation of what was recorded in the Bible, both the New and the Old testaments. The focus was always on God.

Questions regarding the trials of daily life dominated, as in the case of one woman who wanted to leave her husband because he was cruel to her. The Virgin Mary answered: *Let her remain close to him and accept her suffering. Jesus, Himself, also suffered.* The answer was startling in a world that has fallen blindly into accepting divorce—the ultimate destruction of family—as falling into the same casual category as a change in one's job.

But curiosity still prevailed. People wanted to know mundane details about things of the world. Were "flying saucers" real? Would there be a third world war? After one session with such questions, the Virgin told two of the visionaries, *Don't ask useless questions dictated by curiosity. The most important thing is to pray, my angels.*

There were also constant questions concerning faiths: Why are there so many different faiths? Are all religions the same? In a region simmering with hatred for those of divergent religious beliefs, the answers were startlingly direct and profound: *Members of all faiths are equal before God. . . . God rules over each faith just like a sovereign rules over his kingdom. . . . In the world, all religions are not the same because all people have not complied with the commandments of God. They reject and disparage them.*

Immediately, skeptics of the apparitions, as well as leaders of the regional religious factions, challenged these responses and used them as evidence that this so-called supernatural event was not from God. The response indicated that all religions are the same, they said. But the visionaries quickly corrected these misconceptions, after presenting them to the Blessed Virgin. She was saying that all people of all faiths are equal before God, not that all faiths are the same. How can people live the messages, she was saying, if they do not respect all people regardless of their beliefs?

The antagonists pressed on: Does this mean all churches are the same and are accepted by God? Her answer: *In some, the strength of prayer to God is greater, in others, smaller. That depends on the priests who motivate others to pray. It depends also on the power which they have.*

At the further urging of priests and theologians, the visionaries asked the Blessed Virgin if she is the Mother of God and if she went to heaven before or after her death. Again, she answered directly: *I am the Mother of God and the Queen of Peace. I went to Heaven before death.* They asked about another sticky point of debate between faiths: Are there other intermediaries besides Jesus between God and man? *There is only one mediator between God and man, and it is Jesus Christ.*

This was a period of rapid spiritual growth for the visionaries, their families, the villagers, and the authorities of the Church. They were gaining so much information! Could this really be from heaven? Even with all that had occurred, many priests did not think so. Meanwhile, the Serb-dominated civil authorities remained convinced that the Medjugorje events were simply a Croatian ploy that would lead to full insurrection against the government.

It was the best and worst of times for all involved.

And it shall come to pass afterward, that I will pour out my spirit on all flesh; your sons and your daughters shall prophesy, your old men shall dream dreams, and your young men shall see visions. Even upon the menservants and the maidservants in those days, I will pour out my spirit. And I will give portents in the heavens and on the earth, blood, fire, and columns of smoke. —JOEL 2:28-30.

6

Signs of Confirmation

As if it were not enough for God to send the Blessed Virgin to appear in daily apparition and to deliver profound teachings through her messages, He provided numerous supernatural signs in and around Medjugorje. And these signs were not reserved just for the visionaries: Many villagers and visiting pilgrims saw them. These little "gifts" were given, according to the Virgin, to "reawaken people's faith."

One of the earliest of these signs did involve the visionaries. On their first day of conversation with the Blessed Virgin, the children ran up the side of the hill to where she appeared, at a rate of speed far exceeding normal physical ability. Vicka was barefoot, yet the sharp-edged stones along the pathway did not cut her feet. Young Jakov knelt on a thorn-covered bush, and the others were sure he would be terribly hurt. Afterwards, he was unharmed.

Many of the villagers, and, later, others who came from throughout the region, would be able to see the three bursts of light that always preceded the Virgin's appearance. On the third day of the apparitions, this light covered not only the spot on the hill where the Virgin appeared, but also the village and the entire region. The light was seen by thousands of people.

Another amazing sign concerning this supernatural light occurred as the apparitions continued into their seventh day. In an attempt to stop the apparitions, the Communist authorities devised a plan to remove the visionaries from the normal apparition site. Two social workers from Citluk were sent by local officials to persuade the visionaries to go for a ride with them through the surrounding area. Since the visionaries knew them personally, they agreed to go. The hidden motive was to keep the visionaries away from the hill past the usual time of the Virgin's appearance, so there would be no apparition.

As the time approached, the visionaries realized what was happening. They became upset and threatened to jump from the moving vehicle. Alarmed, the social workers stopped on the side of a road and allowed the visionaries to get out of the vehicle. Looking toward the village, the social workers, along with the visionaries, witnessed a light that was illuminating the mountainside of the apparitions. The light then suddenly began moving toward them and settled over the visionaries as they knelt in ecstasy on the side of the road for their daily encounter with the Virgin.

There were other wondrous signs of light. Twenty days after the apparitions began, thousands saw a startling sign in the sky. In sharp cloud formation, the Croatian word for peace, "MIR," appeared and stayed for a long period of time, hovering over the large cross on Krizevac Mountain. This and other phenomena involved the rugged cross that overlooked the valley.

The Blessed Virgin told the visionaries that she prayed to her Son early each morning at the foot of this cross. Several times the cross was observed to disappear totally from view for a period of time, then reappear. It also seemed to spin or rotate on its axis after reappearing.[3]

Again, as if this sign were not enough, the greatest and most commonly seen sign would be what has become known as the "miracle of the sun." This sign first occurred during the final apparition of the Virgin Mary in Fatima, Portugal, on October 13, 1917 (more details about this apparition will be given later). In excess of 70,000 people were witnesses that day, many of them reporting that the sun seemed suddenly to begin spinning, moving about, and throwing off colors of the rainbow. It then seemed to dance around, and swoop down close to the panicking people. Later, a variety of religious images were seen to form around it. This stunning, unbelievable display caused many of the witnesses to think that the end of the world was upon them.

It may be that this was God's intention. Here is the most stable body in the sky suddenly abandoning the laws of physics. Such an occurance was an impossibility; believer and unbeliever alike were left without explanation. For the "Woman clothed with the sun" (Revelation 12:1), this was the perfect sign to tell humanity that God indeed was speaking directly to them through her supernatural appearances.

The same phenomenon was witnessed in Medjugorje for the first time on August 2, 1981. Approximately 150 people saw it while on Podbrdo Hill, the place where the Virgin had first appeared. Just as the sun was about to set, it suddenly seemed to come toward them and then to recede and begin spinning on its axis. People were able to look directly at the sun without injury to their eyes. At the end, a large white cloud came upon the hillside and settled over the sun, which then returned to its normal state. The entire phenomenon lasted approximately fifteen minutes.

One witness gave this report: "I was with a large group of people outside the church and suddenly, I noticed the sun doing strange things. It began to swing from side to side, then a ray of light separated itself from the sun and traveled like the rays of a rainbow towards the place where the Virgin had first appeared. It then rested on the church tower, on which a clear image of the Virgin appeared."

This would be the first of hundreds of occurences of the miracle of the sun over the years of the daily apparitions.

For the visionaries and the followers of the messages, it was no coincidence that this sign of the sun first occurred on August 2, the Feast of Our Lady, Queen of the Angels. Many of the people witnessing the miracle on this day reported seeing large globules of light of various colors, moving around the sun. They also reported seeing images of the Blessed Virgin and a great number of angels with trumpets coming out of the sun. Then, according to some, a large heart was seen, and under it, six small hearts, images that were taken as representing the Virgin and the six young visionaries.

Near the end of the first year of apparitions, many people saw the huge cross on the top of Krizevac Mountain transform itself into a brilliant, shimmering light and then into a silhouette of the Blessed Virgin Mary. The visionaries were urged to ask the Virgin explain this and the other signs. This was her reply: *All of these signs are designed to strengthen your faith until I leave you the visible and permanent sign.*

What was this permanent sign? the visionaries were asked. They explained that the Virgin had told them the permanent sign would be the greatest of the supernatural signs in Medjugorje. They added that they had been shown this sign in the course of the apparitions. When the sign is given, they said, it will be left permanently on the hill at the very spot where the first apparition took place. The sign will be visible to everyone and will be proof that these apparitions are indeed from God. It will be able to be photographed, televised, and seen—but not touched. When questioned about it not being able to be touched, the visionaries were not clear if this meant it would be forbidden to touch it, or that it would be impossible to touch it because of its composition.

As to when it will occur, the date is only known to the visionaries, who say that it is one of three warnings that will be given to the world sometime after the apparitions cease occurring daily. There is no set date or indication of just how soon the warnings will be given once the apparitions are over.

The Virgin later added this about the permanent sign: *The sign will come, but you must not spend too much time looking for it. My urgent message to you is, be converted! Pass this message to all my children wherever they are. There is no trouble I will not take, no suffering I will not bear to save them. I shall beg my Son not to punish the world, but I implore you, be converted, change your lives. You cannot begin to imagine what lies ahead . . . so, I beg you again, be converted!*

Again, she stresses the importance of living the messages in daily life. What would any of us do if we knew the exact date the permanent sign would be given, or what the future chastisements might be? Would we not pray, fast, and do penance as the messages urge us constantly to do?

If the permanent sign was to become the greatest of the phenomena, one of the most common would be the change in color, from silver to gold, of the metal links of rosaries of pilgrims. Sometimes the metal would change color as the pilgrim was praying the prayers of the rosary. Old rosaries would change color just as frequently as new ones, and occasionally, the process would be reversed, with gold color metal changing to a silver color. Some skeptics took the investigation to a higher scientific level by having the changed metal tested by qualified jewelers. In some cases, they were shocked to discover that the coating on the metal was actually gold!

Another startling sign took place after an apparition at Jakov's home in late October. The letters "MIR LJUDIMA" (Peace to the people) appeared in a brilliant gold color on one of the walls in his house. This was again an underlining of the Blessed Virgin's call for the people to reconcile with one another. She continued, sometimes gently and at other times with extreme somberness, to warn them to seek peace through prayer.

Shortly after the day this sign had appeared on the wall, the visionaries were praying together when suddenly, the Virgin intervened: *Oh my Son, Jesus, forgive these sins; there are so many of them!* They paused and became silent, and she added, *Continue to pray, because prayer is the salvation of the people.*

Regardless of the many signs and wonders accompanying the daily appearances of the Blessed Virgin Mary, strong skeptics remained, including many priests. Ivan asked the Virgin how to help doubting priests understand the apparitions. She answered directly: *It is necessary to tell them that from the very beginning I have been conveying the message of God to the world. It is a great pity not to believe in it. Faith is a vital element, but one cannot compel a person to believe. Faith is the foundation from which everything flows.*

As if the apparitions alone were not enough, the Spirit was being poured out in abundance to allow every possible opportunity for individual conversion.

. . . How shall we escape if we neglect such a great salvation? It was declared at first by the Lord, and it was attested to us by those who heard him, while God also bore witness by signs and wonders and various miracles and by gifts of the Holy Spirit distributed according to his own will. —HEBREWS 2:3.

7
Storm Warning

Another important sign was given on the first day of the apparitions. This sign, an ominous one, did not come through the intercession of the Blessed Virgin Mary, but from the one who always comes to counteract her mission. It would later be recognized as an important sign of confirmation of Medjugorje's apparitions. Sadly, it would be the one most ignored, for that inattention the people of the region would pay a horrible price.

The ominous sign came suddenly in the early morning hours of June 24, 1981, as a full-fury summer storm enveloped the valley in minutes, turning the calm of night into unholy terror. The storm raged at maximum intensity. Many villagers, startled out of a deep sleep by ear-splitting peals of thunder and continuous streaks of lightning, were certain doomsday had arrived.

Torrents of hard rain were driven sideways by furious gusts of wind; lightning struck the post office and set it afire.

Claps of thunder caused the ground to shake as though struck by an earthquake. The storm subsided as quickly as it had come, leaving the villagers shaken as they fought the raging fire at the post office.

Only later would these sudden minutes of dark fury be seen as an ominous calling card of the Prince of Darkness, there to do battle again with the Woman sent by heaven.

Approximately 16 hours later, Ivanka first saw the Blessed Virgin on the hillside. The formation of another battle in the age-old clash between good and evil began to unfold; the new battlefield was the tiny village of Medjugorje.

Now, two months later, on August 2, the same day the miracle of the sun was first witnessed in Medjugorje, a strange event took place late that evening. After the Mass, a small group of villagers gathered with the visionaries in an isolated field away from the church to sing and pray in honor of the feast day (Our Lady of the Angels, as mentioned in the preceding chapter). The Virgin suddenly appeared without notice to the visionaries. Marija startled the gathering when she suddenly announced, "Our Lady says she will allow those who so desire to come and touch her."

As the people rushed forward to "touch" the Virgin, the visionaries would tell them: "You are touching her veil . . . now you are touching her head . . . her dress." Suddenly Marija shouted: "Oh! Our Lady is disappearing and she is completely blackened!"

Marija's neighbor Marinko Ivankovic, a stalwart defender and protector of the children from the first days of the apparitions, asked Marija what had happened. "Oh, Marinko," she replied, "there were sinners here and as they touched her, her dress got darker and darker until it turned black." Marija then asked that all present go to confession the following day.

Appalled by this visible evidence of the power of sin, Marinko loudly echoed Marija's call for confession, making sure all were aware of it. He then learned in further conversation with Marija that another unusual and unannounced apparition had occurred earlier. As Marija was preparing to go to the field, the Virgin suddenly appeared to her in her room, telling her, *The devil is trying to infiltrate himself here in order to get something. My Son wants to win over all the souls, but the devil is exerting himself to get something. He is making every effort and wants at any price to infiltrate among you.*

"I am not sure if Marija understood Our Lady correctly or not," Marinko was later quoted, "but she stated that Our Lady also said that she does not know how all of this will turn out, if the devil will succeed or not. . . ."

Was the Virgin referring to her warning about the devil wanting to infiltrate among the visionaries, or about Medjugorje as a whole? The answer to that question was not clear. However, there was little doubt from her unusual added apparitions to Marija on this special feast day, or from her words, that the battle was on. Without the people's response to her pleadings for prayer, fasting, and penance, the outcome would remain unclear. Response could only come by the free-will choice of good over evil.

The next day there were long lines in and around the church for confession. And the following day there were still more. The numbers of the confessions and their intensity astounded the priests who heard them. Pleased with the response, the Virgin urged the people through the visionaries to continue on a path of repentance and conversion.

Shortly after this event, another major development in the brief history of the apparitions was revealed: The visionaries disclosed to the priests that the Virgin was giving them secrets concerning the future. According to them, she would reveal progressively to each of them ten future events that would occur in the world. They were not to divulge these events, or secrets as they were called, to anyone until given permission by the Virgin—not even to the Franciscans or to family members. Once a visionary had received all ten secrets, the Virgin would no longer appear on a daily basis to that particular visionary.

The only detail concerning the secrets revealed at the time was that the permanent sign was the third of three warnings that would be given shortly after the last visionary ceased to receive the apparitions (as explained in an earlier chapter). Later, Mirjana would add this about the permanent sign: "When the permanent sign appears, unbelievers will run to the hill and pray for forgiveness. . . ."

While the Virgin emphasized that attention to the ten secrets should be minimal—that is, know about them, but focus primarily on her direct messages, which lead to daily conversion—one can assume some details based on various statements by the visionaries. The first three secrets appear to be warnings given to the world to prove that the apparitions are truly from God. The next three future event messages seem to concern specifically the village and the visionaries personally, perhaps with different secrets for the individual visionaries. And the last four seem clearly to do with chastisements that will occur in the world.[4]

Some reassurance was given later when the Virgin said that because of the prayers, fasting, and penance of those responding to her call, the seventh secret, or chastisement, had been mitigated. Other chastisements can also be mitigated, she revealed through Mirjana, but the tenth will occur, because "everyone will not convert."

Mirjana revealed later that Satan had appeared to her during this time to try to sway her away from her devotion to the Blessed Virgin Mary. She claimed that one evening, as she prepared for her daily apparition, there was suddenly a flash of light and he appeared. She described him as "horrible and black all over, terrifying." She then passed out momentarily, awakening, she said, to "find him standing there, laughing . . . he told me I would be very beautiful and very happy in love and life, and so on, but that I would have no need of the Madonna or of my faith. . . . Then something inside of me shouted, No! I began to shake and to feel sick and then he disappeared, and the Madonna came, telling me that it would not happen again . . ."

Later, the Blessed Virgin would add this message: *The Devil tries to impose his power on you, but you must remain strong and persevere in your faith. You must pray and fast. I will always be close to you.*

The visionaries, the Church, and the villagers would need that reassurance. The storm warning was over, but the battle was just beginning.

I will put enmity between you and the woman, and between your seed and her seed; he shall bruise your head, and you shall bruise his heel. —GENESIS 3:15.

PART II

Planting

First of all you must understand this, that scoffers will come in the
last days with scoffing, following their own passions and saying,
"Where is the promise of His coming? For ever since the fathers fell
asleep, all things have continued as they were from the beginning of
creation." . . . But do not ignore this fact, beloved. . . . The Lord is
not slow about His promise as some count slowness, but is forbearing
toward you, not wishing that any should perish but that all should
reach repentance. But the Day of the Lord
will come like a thief in the night.
—2 PETER 3:3–10.

8

Nurturing Grace

What was happening in Medjugorje was similar to the events that occurred in other places where the Virgin Mary came in apparition in past times of crisis. Such occurrences dot the pages of history, giving ongoing evidence of God's constant nurturing through the outpouring of His grace.

The Virgin seems to be sent as special messenger in certain times of extreme crisis to give warnings and guidance directly from heaven. Her appearances are actually a continuation of the precedent set in the pages of the Old Testament when God raised up prophets in times of urgent need. The modern era is no different, especially with the state of the contemporary world.

The earliest recorded apparition of the Virgin Mary of modern times occurred in England at Walsingham in 1061 (discussed in a later chapter), while one of the most mystical took place at Guadalupe (today, Mexico City), in 1531. The Guadalupe visionary was a 57-year-old, recently converted

Indian named Juan Diego, who was instructed by the Virgin to tell the bishop that she wished a chapel to be built on the spot where she was appearing.

When the bishop expressed doubt, the Virgin appeared to Juan again and, after picking an assortment of beautiful roses—which could not possibly be blooming at that time of year—she meticulously arranged them inside his tilma, a cloak made out of cactus weed. She then carefully folded it and told him to take them to the bishop.

As Juan Diego opened the cloak to show the flowers, the bishop fell to his knees, his eyes transfixed on the tilma, which now bore a full color image of the Virgin as a beautiful young Indian woman. The tilma, which normally would last approximately 30 to 40 years before disintegration, remains on display in Mexico City, still bearing the image of the Virgin Mary in brilliant color after nearly 500 years. The apparitions at Guadalupe eventually led to the conversion of seven million pagans, and lead ultimately to the formation of the nation of Mexico.

Based on the content of the messages, the beginning of the present era of apparitions of the Blessed Virgin can be pinpointed to the little village of La Salette, France, located in the Alps. La Salette was a skimpily populated collection of hamlets, not unlike Medjugorje. The Virgin appeared only one time, on Saturday, September 19, 1846, to two young children who were serving as shepherds hired by local ranchers.

Melanie Mathieu, 14, and Maximin Giraud, 11, were checking on the animals when suddenly they saw a large circle of brilliant light in the ravine below. Running towards it, they watched as it began to open, revealing the figure of a woman surrounded by light. She was seated with her face in her hands, crying. As they moved nearer she arose, opened her arms and began speaking to them in perfect French:

Come to me, my children, do not be afraid; I am here to tell you something of great importance.

The children looked at each other, puzzled, as they did not clearly understand her words: Simple peasants, they spoke a regional dialect. The woman in the light then changed to their patois and repeated the greeting. After identifying herself, she gave Maximin a secret message. She then turned to Melanie and gave a long message, to be kept secret until 1858. Parts of that message are as follows: *The priests, my Son's ministers, by their bad lives, their irreverence and impiety in celebrating the Sacred Mysteries, by love of money, love of honor and pleasures, the priests have become cesspools of impurity. . . . The heads, the leaders of the people of God, have neglected prayer and penance, and the devil has darkened their intelligence. . . . Bad books will abound upon the earth, the spirits of darkness will propagate a universal falling off everywhere in all that concerns the service of God. They will have great power over nature. There will be churches where the spirits are served. . . .*

The Virgin then turned her attention to the world in general: *God is going to strike in an unprecedented manner. Woe to the inhabitants of the earth! There will be a general war which will be dreadful* (World War I). *. . . Nature cries out for vengeance upon mankind and groans in terror in apprehension of what must come upon the earth, so sullied with crimes. . . . Before this happens there will be a sort of false peace in the world. People will think only of amusing themselves. The wicked will lend themselves to all sorts of sins. . . .*

Does this not sound like the world today? The message ends, however, with a consoling call for return to God, including these words: *I address an urgent appeal to the earth: I summon the true disciples of God who lives and reigns in heaven. I summon the true imitators of Christ the God-Man. . . .*

The reaction to such a phenomenon at that time was the same as it is today—disbelief and a lack of interest by clergy and laity alike. Yet, the intent was the same as that manifested at Medjugorje, namely to lead the people back to God.

Nearly seventy years later, on May 13, 1917, the Virgin Mary came for the people of the twentieth century. She began appearing in the little town of Fatima, Portugal. Once again, the world was in a time of grave crisis. World War I was threatening to bring an end to civilization, just as the Virgin had predicted at La Salette; this was also a time of tremendous religious, social, and political upheaval. Russia was in chaos. And in Portugal, the Christian faith was challenged to the point of extinction by a Marxist-leaning government.

Into this setting came the mother of Jesus—again. And again, she came to peasant children: Lucia, a devout girl of ten, her cousins Francisco, age nine, and little seven-year-old Jacinta. The similarity to La Salette continues as the young children were tending sheep in the hills when the Virgin first appeared on the thirteenth day of May 1917; she would appear to them on the thirteenth of the month for the next five months, with the final apparition coming in October.

During the course of the appearances, the children were given messages, were taught to pray and, much to their surprise, were shown vivid scenes of hell. In scenes that were to be repeated in the first days of the Medjugorje events, they were subjected to ridicule and harassment by the authorities, both civil and religious.

There were also great signs given to prove that the Virgin was truly appearing. The most noticeable was the first recorded miracle of the sun, as reported earlier. In a dazzling display seen in the midst of a violent rainstorm, the sun seemed to move about the sky, spinning and dancing and appearing to come directly at the people. Many were convinced that they were seeing the end of the world. Most convincing was the fact that a crowd numbering more than 70,000, including skeptics and journalists, witnessed the phenomenon firsthand. Thousands more saw it in areas surrounding the sight as far as fifty miles away.

Amazingly, when the miracle of the sun at Fatima ended, the skies were clear, the sun shone brightly, and all present were suddenly dry and free of the mud that had previously caked their clothing. Believers and unbelievers alike were astonished.

As at La Salette, powerful messages were given to the young visionaries. The Virgin gave special messages to Lucia and stressed the prayers of the rosary as a powerful prayer to fulfill her requests. After the Virgin showed the children a vision of hell, the frightened children raised their eyes to the Virgin, who told them: *You saw Hell where the souls of poor sinners go. In order to save them God wishes to establish in the world devotion to my Immaculate Heart. If people do what I ask, many souls will be saved and there will be peace. The war* (World War I) *is going to end. But if people do not stop offending God, another, even worse, will begin in the reign of Pius XI.*

Thus, the Virgin predicted World War II, marked by a sign that she also predicted when she told the children that at a time in the future there would be a light seen around the world. That sign occurred in 1939 through a worldwide strange light in the sky, a light that many reported as resembling the aurora borealis. But according to Lucia in an interview years later, it was not the aurora borealis, but a specific phenomenon as predicted by the Virgin Mary. In her 1917 prediction, the Virgin also added, . . . *If people attend to my requests, Russia will be converted and the world will have peace. If not, Russia will spread its errors throughout the world, fomenting wars and persecutions of the Church. . . .*"

The chaos then occurring in Russia developed into revolution, leading to the political development of Communism and its subsequent spread throughout the world. A little more than 70 years later, Communism would collapse without a new revolution or a war, and without sufficient worldly explanation. Once again, the Virgin Mary at Fatima predicted Communism's demise. This prediction was further assurance to the young visionaries that in the end, the Virgin's Immaculate Heart would triumph.

Stated simply, the peace and love of God would eventually win the battle against evil, and that triumph would be part of the conclusion of Medjugorje's apparitions.

To Lucia, the Blessed Virgin gave what has come to be known as the Third Secret of Fatima. This secret is actually a continuation of the above message; this particular part of the message was not to be revealed by the hierarchy of the Catholic Church until 1960. However, when the time came that the secret could be revealed, the Church officials chose not to do so out of concern for public reaction to its contents.

More than sixty years after the apparitions at Fatima, the Virgin began to appear at Medjugorje. Now a cloistered nun in Portugal, Lucia is the only living visionary of Fatima. The Virgin had told her in 1917 that she would live to see the Triumph of her Immaculate Heart. It is reported that upon hearing about Medjugorje, Lucia exclaimed that Medjugorje is the fulfillment of the secrets of Fatima.

Adding further credence to this ongoing era of supernatural communications is another series of messages that play a major role in this spiritual drama. They have run concurrent to the Medjugorje apparitions, with the exception of having started nine years earlier.

In May 1972 an Italian priest named Stefano Gobbi was taking part in a pilgrimage to Fatima. As he prayed for certain priests who had left the priesthood and were forming a rebellious group to challenge Church authority, he suddenly felt an interior presence of the Virgin Mary. From that moment onward, he began receiving by interior locution[5] messages from her. This series of ongoing messages was designed to recruit a large army of priests for these end times.

For more than 25 years, Father Gobbi traveled the globe speaking at assemblies of priests about the Virgin's messages, and conducting prayer gatherings known as "cenacles." Today, close to 4,000 priests, including 20 bishops, are members of the Marian Movement of Priests. The public cenacles came to an end in 1998, as the Blessed Virgin stated that *All has been revealed to you. . . .*

Again, it is no accident that this phenomenon began at Fatima. The messages given to Father Gobbi are nearly identical to those of Medjugorje; the exception is that they are more pointed and blunt, as opposed to the simplicity and gentleness of those at Medjugorje. Medjugorje's lessons are meant for the faithful, the children of God. The Marian Movement of Priests is meant to alert the Church in the strongest of terms.

The clear relationship to Fatima in the messages of these two supernatural events can be seen in the message the Virgin gave to Father Gobbi in 1990 at Fatima, not coincidentally, on the anniversary of the Fatima apparitions. On May 13, 1990, Father Gobbi and a group of his fellow priests had gathered in the very place the Virgin appeared in 1917 in Fatima, when Father Gobbi received a message, excerpts of which follow:

I came down from heaven 73 years ago, in this Cova da Iria, to point out for you the path you should tread in the course of this difficult century of yours. . . . Humanity has not accepted my motherly request to return to the Lord along the road of conversion of heart and of life, of prayer and of penance. Thus, it has known terrible years of the second world war, which brought about tens of millions of deaths and vast destruction of populaces and of nations. . . . Satan has been the uncontested dominator of the events of this century of yours, bringing all humanity to the rejection of God and of His law of love, spreading far and wide division and hatred, immorality and wickedness, and legitimating everywhere divorce, abortion, obscenity, homosexuality and recourse to any and all means of obstructing life. . . . I am coming down from heaven (now in these times), *so that the final secrets may be revealed to you and that I may be able thus to prepare you for what, as of now, you must live through, for the purification of the earth. . . .*

Always the loving mother, the Blessed Virgin ended the message on a note of hope:

Humanity will live through the moment of its great chastisement and thus will be made ready to receive the Lord Jesus who will return to you in glory. . . .

She concluded with these words:

For this reason, especially today, I am coming down again from heaven: through my numerous apparitions; through the messages which I give; and, through this extraordinary work of my Marian Movement of Priests, to prepare you to live through the events which are even now in the process of being fulfilled, in order to lead you by the hand to walk along the most difficult and painful segment of this your second advent, and to prepare the minds and the hearts of all to receive Jesus at the closely approaching moment of His glorious return.

In short, Medjugorje is a continuation of the apparitions of the Blessed Virgin at Fatima. The messages given by interior locution to the founder of the Marian Movement of Priests are further confirmation of that fact. As with La Salette, the messages are virtually the same in general content. The Blessed Virgin comes with gentleness and urgency, tinged with loving concern for her children as any human mother would.

As she had done with the visionaries at Fatima, the Blessed Virgin took each Medjugorje visionary to—or allowed them to see by vision—heaven, hell, and purgatory. In early October, Vicka was at Jakov's home when the Virgin suddenly appeared and told them that she was going to take them to see heaven. Jakov, frightened and thinking they would not return, said, "Why don't you just take Vicka. She has many brothers and sisters, but I am the only child of my mother."

The Virgin smiled and took the two of them by the hand; in a flash, they were in heaven. Jakov's mother would report afterward that they completely disappeared from the house for a period of approximately 20 minutes. Vicka later described heaven as a wonderfully beautiful place, filled with a sense of peace and happiness that made them want to stay and not return to earthly life. She said that it was filled with people dressed in pastel-colored gowns with no one older than 33 years of age. After showing them this part of paradise and telling them not to be afraid, the Virgin said: *All those who are faithful to God will have that.*

All the visionaries described purgatory as a place of gray-brown mist, where they did not see anyone but felt anguish and a yearning for peace. Vicka would also describe hell: It was a place of fire and darkness. She reported witnessing vividly a blonde teenage girl going into the flames of hell, shrieking and cursing God, coming out blackened and looking like an animal, and continuing to curse God.

The visionaries questioned the Virgin about her reasons for showing them these places, especially paradise. *I did that so you could see the happiness which awaits those who love God.*

During one apparition, Jesus appeared suddenly to them, with injuries covering His body and a crown of thorns pressing on His head. The Virgin comforted them: *Do not be afraid. It is my Son. See how He has been martyred. In spite of all, He was joyful and He endured all with patience.* Then she added: *I am often at Krizevac, at the foot of the cross, to pray there. Now I pray to my Son to forgive the world its sins. The world has begun to convert.*

During this apparition, the Virgin disappeared and the visionaries again saw a terrifying vision of hell. She then reappeared and said: *Do not be afraid! I have shown you Hell so that you may know the state of those who are there.* She added, *The devil is trying to conquer us. Do not permit him. Keep the faith, fast, and pray. I will be with you at every step.*

The Virgin was indescribably beautiful as light radiated, flowed, shined, and sparkled around her. She again added, *The people have begun to convert. Keep a solid faith. I need your prayers.*

Thus, from the many examples of the Blessed Virgin Mary coming in apparition through the past two centuries, we have seen the Divine Creator pouring out grace always on human creation. Now at Medjugorje, He would continue, once again choosing as a vessel a human mother, the one selected to bring Him, the only-begotten Son, into the world.

And when Elizabeth heard the greeting of Mary, the babe leaped in her womb; and Elizabeth was filled with the Holy Spirit and she exclaimed with a loud cry, "Blessed are you among women, and blessed is the fruit of your womb! And why is this granted me, that the mother of my Lord should come to me?" —LUKE 1:41-42.

9
Cultivation

With every encounter, the Virgin implored the visionaries, and the pilgrims through them, to focus on the content of the grace she was bringing them through her messages. Her emphasis was always on the need to pray, fast, and do penance in order to fulfill God's plan at Medjugorje. She reminded them again of the threat of Satan: *Satan only says what he wants. He interferes in everything. You, my angels, be ready to endure everything. Here, many things will take place. Do not allow yourselves to be surprised by him.*

The visionaries were frequently given questions, especially theological questions, to ask the Virgin. The Virgin responded, with explicit information. To one inquiry concerning purgatory, she answered: *There are many souls in Purgatory. There are also persons* (there) *who have been consecrated to God—some priests, some religious. Pray for their intentions, at least the Lord's Prayer, the Hail Mary, and the Glory Be seven times each, and the Creed. I recommend it to you. There is a large number of souls who have been in Purgatory for a long time because no one prays for them.*

In another message, Ivanka was given this word about purgatory: *In Purgatory there are different levels; the lowest is close to Hell and the highest gradually draws near to Heaven. It is not on All Souls Day, but at Christmas, that the greatest number of souls leave Purgatory. There are in Purgatory, souls who pray ardently to God, but for whom no relative or friend prays on earth. God makes them benefit from the prayers of other people. It happens that God permits them to manifest themselves in different ways, close to their relatives on earth, in order to remind men of the existence of Purgatory and to solicit their prayers to come close to God who is just, but good. The majority of people go to Purgatory. Many go to Hell. A small number go directly to Heaven.*

Some people were disturbed that someone who was "bad" all his life could suddenly repent and be loved by God. At one person's request the visionaries asked the Virgin about being bad all one's life and asking forgiveness. She replied: *Whoever has done very much evil during his life can go straight to Heaven if he confesses, is sorry for what he has done, and receives Communion at the end of his life.* Just as the good thief crucified with Jesus repented on the cross, and was told he would be in heaven that very day. . . .

And concerning hell for those who do not repent: *Today many persons go to Hell. God allows His children to suffer in Hell due to the fact that they have committed grave, unpardonable sins. Those who are in Hell no longer have a chance to know a lot better.*

Other answers stated that people who commit grave sins live in hell while still on earth and continue this hell in eternity, meaning they reject God completely, and consciously choose evil as a lifestyle. They actually go to hell because they chose hell in life, and again at the moment of death.

Mirjana shared with her spiritual advisor that she had developed an overwhelming maternal love for and intimacy with the Virgin. For that reason she could not understand how any soul could choose to go to hell. She questioned Gospa as to why God could send sinners so "mercilessly" to hell forever. The Virgin answered with gentleness, *Men who go to Hell no longer want to receive any benefit from God. They do not repent nor do they cease to revolt and to blaspheme. They make up their mind to live in Hell and do not contemplate leaving it.*

The Virgin gave this revelation about heaven and reincarnation: *You go to Heaven in full conscience—that which you have now. At the moment of death, you are conscious of the separation of the body and soul. It is false to teach people that you are reborn many times and that you pass to different bodies. One is born only once. The body, drawn from the earth, decomposes after death. It never comes back to life again. Man receives a transfigured body.*

There were constant questions about and requests for cures. To one such question, the Virgin replied: *For the cure of the sick, it is important to say the following prayers: the Creed, and seven times each, the Lord's Prayer, the Hail Mary, and the Glory Be, and to fast on bread and water. It is good to impose one's hands on the sick and to pray. It is good to anoint the sick with Holy oil. All priests do not have the gift of healing. In order to receive this gift, the priest must pray with perseverance and believe firmly.*

The sequence of prayers just mentioned, taught to the visionaries in the first days of the apparitions, seems to be a formula recommended frequently by the Blessed Virgin. She returns constantly to the basic fundamentals of the grace of her visits. It is through prayer and fasting that heaven responds.

How do we fast? Who must fast, and what is the best way? To these questions, the Virgin gave this reply: *The best fast is on bread and water. Through fasting and prayer, one can stop wars, one can suspend the laws of nature. Charity cannot replace fasting. Those who are not able to fast can sometime replace it with prayer, charity, and a confession; but everyone, except the sick, must fast.*

By requesting fasting, the Virgin was asking for the people to give God a gift. Sometimes the gift might be large, and at other times it might be small. Some days we are able to fast on bread and water, and other days, we cannot; on those days, the gift is smaller. What is important, she emphasized, is that we attempt to give a gift. If one cannot fast on bread and water, for example, due to sickness or a handicap, one can give up normal pleasures, such as television, shopping, sweets, etc. That gift, combined with prayers, can then be "used" to help others for specific needs, or to bring them into ongoing spirituality.

The Virgin made a similar point concerning confession: *One must invite people to go to Confession each month, especially the first Saturday.*[6] *Here, I have not spoken of it yet. I have invited people to frequent Confession. I will give you yet some concrete messages for our time. Be patient because the time has not yet come. Do what I have told you. They are numerous who do not observe it. Monthly Confession will be a remedy for the Church in the West. One must convey this message to the West.*

As to her role as a messenger from heaven, she said, *I do not dispose all graces. I receive from God what I obtain through prayer. God has placed His complete trust in me. I particularly protect those who have been consecrated to me.*

The great sign has been granted. It will appear independently of the conversion of the people.

On the question of praying to her, the Virgin Mary made clear her role and that of other saints: *Jesus prefers that you address yourselves directly to Him rather than through an intermediary. In the meantime, if you wish to give yourselves completely to God and if you wish that I be your protector, then confide to me all your intentions, your fasts, and your sacrifices so that I can dispose of them according to the will of God.* In other words, she can serve as an intercessor, just as we ask one another to pray for our needs.

Many questions were asked concerning the world: Would there be a third world war? *The third world war will not take place.* What will happen in Poland where the people have been fighting for freedom for so long? *There will be great conflicts, but in the end, the just will take over.* And what about Russia? *The Russian people will be the people who will glorify God the most. The West has made civilization progress, but without God, as if they were their own creators.*

In December 1982, there was a sharp change in the routine of the apparitions. For a year and a half, the Virgin had come daily, appearing to each of the six visionaries. As related above, she had told them that she would give each of them ten secrets concerning the future of the world, and upon receiving the tenth, they would no longer see her daily. For Mirjana, that final apparition would come all too soon. In late December, the Virgin told her: *On Christmas, I will appear to you* (daily) *for the last time.*

On that holy day, Mirjana was given the tenth secret, a particularly grave one. And while the Virgin would no longer be appearing daily to her, she promised to appear on Mirjana's birthday, March 18, for the rest of her life, as well as at other times when necessary. The final daily apparition lasted 45 minutes. Mirjana stated that she will always remember these words of the Virgin: *Now you will have to turn to God in the faith like any other person. I will appear to you on the day of your birthday and when you will experience difficulties in life. Mirjana, I have chosen you; I have confided in you everything that is essential. I have shown you many terrible things. You must now bear it all with courage. Think of me and think of the tears I must shed for that. You must remain courageous. You have quickly grasped the messages. You must also understand now that I have to go away. Be courageous.*

It was a sad Christmas for Mirjana. She later reported in an interview: "After she left, I just sat there like a statue, feeling very strange and thinking to myself: 'This can't be happening, she will come back.'"

But she did not come back. After calming down in the next few days, Mirjana added, "Our Lady said that she has stayed with us for longer than necessary, because this is the last time Jesus or she will appear on earth."[7]

It left the five remaining visionaries wondering how much longer the Virgin of Medjugorje would appear to them.

For he will render to every man according to his works: to those who by patience in well doing seek for glory and honor and immortality, he will give eternal life; but for those who do not obey the truth, there will be wrath and fury. —ROMANS 2:6-8.

10
Fertile Soil

Proving again to be the caring mother, the Virgin Mary added a new dimension to the apparitions as they continued into 1983. A ten-year-old girl from the village suddenly began seeing and hearing the Virgin Mary in a manner different from the way the visionaries experienced her. Coming as it did a few days after Mirjana received her final daily apparition, this new manifestation of the Virgin was almost certainly not coincidence. Shortly after this, another young girl the same age began having the same experience.

While in class at school, ten-year-old Jelena Vasilij began to hear a gentle voice speaking to her interiorly. The words were of routine things at first, as though allowing the child to familiarize herself with the process. A few days later, Jelena discovered the "source" of the inner voice: "I saw and heard the angel who prepared me for the coming of Our Lady. . . . He didn't say so, but I knew he was my guardian angel."

The Blessed Virgin came first to Jelena on December 29. She spoke but did not appear to her immediately. When she did appear, she did so in a manner different from the way she appeared to the six visionaries. Jelena described the experience as inner words and visions. She saw "with the heart," whereas the other six saw the same thing with their eyes shut or open. Also, Jelena's locutions occurred two or three times in a day. As the visionaries did, the young girl would prepare with a period of prayer.

Three months later, another ten-year-old, a close friend of Jelena's, who was frequently in prayer with her before her locutions, began experiencing the same charisma. Marijana Vasilij (not related) became the eighth youth in the village to experience the presence of Gospa. She would later describe to a priest how the young locutionists saw her (curiously, different in her manner of coming and attire): "First a white cloud comes that disappears when Our Lady comes. She is all in white and wears a crown of stars held together by themselves without a wire, and a rosary hangs from her folded hands."

Marijana also stated that Jesus sometimes accompanied the Virgin during the interior visions. She described Him as being visible only from the waist up, having long black hair, and wearing a gray robe with a red cape. She added that He was only seen and never spoke during these sessions, although He sometimes smiled.

In May 1983 the Virgin began giving Jelena teachings concerning spiritual life. She told her to write down the teachings because she was to entrust them later to Church authorities. By this time, Jelena, who was the main receiver of the inner locutions, could speak to the Virgin at will—but only on spiritual matters. The Blessed Virgin told her that all she needed to know was written in the Gospels, that she should read and believe them, and that she would find the answers to all her questions in them.

While the mission of these two young locutionists was complementary to that of the six visionaries, they were told that later it would be different. They would not receive the special future event messages (the ten secrets) that were to be given to the visionaries, but they seemed to receive stronger, more detailed messages on spirituality. Still, their role was not quite the same as that of the visionaries.

After four months of preparing the two locutionists, the Virgin asked Jelena to advise her spiritual director that Gospa would like a prayer group comprised of young people to be established in the parish. Those who wished to join the prayer group were asked to commit voluntarily to four years of total consecration to God, putting aside all decisions concerning the future during this time. They were asked to meet three times a week, to pray at least three hours daily, to go to Mass frequently, and to fast on bread and water twice a week. These guidelines would in time become the standard for similar prayer groups that would spring up throughout the world, inspired by the apparitions at Medjugorje.

The first meeting of the prayer group took place in the basement of the rectory on a Tuesday evening. It was no coincidence that the Virgin's first message to the group was to love their enemies: *I know that you are not able to love your enemies, but I beg you to pray every day at least five minutes to the Sacred Heart, and to my Heart, and we will give you the divine love with which you will be able to love even your enemies.*

As had been the case in the first year and a half of apparitions, the Blessed Virgin was again emphasizing prayer as a pathway to learning spiritual love. And again, she pointedly reminded the people of the ethnic divisions within the region. Such a message was especially important to the young, who were potentially more capable of changing traditional hatreds than adults, who had them ingrained from decades of conflict.

The young prayer group grew in spiritual intensity and in numbers. Two months later, the Virgin told the group: *You have decided to follow Jesus, to consecrate yourselves totally to Him. Now, when a person decides to follow God totally, Satan comes along and tries to remove that person from the path on which they have set out. This is the time of testing. He will try by all means to lead you astray. Satan will tell you: "This is too much. This is nonsense. You can be Christians like everybody else. Don't pray, don't fast." I tell you, this is the time when you must persevere in your fast and your prayers. You must not listen to Satan. Do what I have told you. Satan can do nothing to those who believe in God and have totally abandoned themselves to him. But you are inexperienced and so I urge you to be careful.*

As the year progressed, Ivan, Jakov, Marija, and Vicka related the following information to their spiritual director: Marija had received seven of the promised ten secrets, Vicka had received eight, while Jakov, Ivanka, and Ivan had each received nine. Mirjana had received all ten and, of course, no longer had daily apparitions.

For many of the pilgrims coming to the village, the main focus was still on the external—the signs and wonders—more so than on the content of the messages. It seemed that almost daily the visionaries were asked about the permanent sign. Again, the Virgin relayed information about the permanent sign: *The sign will come, you must not worry about it. The only thing that I would want to tell you is to be converted.*

Make that known to all my children as quickly as possible. No pain, no suffering is too great for me in order to save you. I will pray to my Son not to punish the world; but I plead with you, be converted. You cannot imagine what is going to happen nor what the Eternal Father will send to earth. That is why you must be converted! Renounce everything. Do penance. Express my thanks to all my children who have prayed and fasted. I carry all this to my Divine Son in order to obtain an alleviation of His justice against the sins of mankind. I thank the people who have prayed and fasted. Persevere and help me to convert the world.

The number of priests visiting the village increased constantly, and with them came more serious questions. Regarding inquiries concerning the physical healings taking place at Medjugorje, the Virgin reminded the visionaries again: *I cannot cure. God alone cures. Pray! I will pray with you. Believe firmly. Fast, do penance. I will help you as long as it is in my power to do it. God comes to help everyone. I am not God. I need your sacrifices and your prayers to help me.*

Such messages added dramatically to the credibility of the apparitions. The opposition continued, but in ratio to the conversions taking place daily, it was all but overshadowed. This was especially true among the religious. Adding to their positive impressions was the experience of confession, with many priests spending hours listening to such outpourings of confessors as they had never heard before. Lines of penitents formed all over the outside lawn of Saint James Church and in adjoining open areas. It was the depth and intensity of the confessions that brought acceptance and belief to many priests who had come as skeptics.

The second anniversary of the apparitions, June 25, 1983, passed with little fanfare and with no special message given by the Virgin to mark the event. However, the visionaries did reveal that she was recounting the story of her life to them, although they could not release the story until she gave her permission. Apparently chosen as the main recipient of the Virgin's life story, Vicka recorded the story for almost four months, filling three notebooks in the process.

During this period the diocesan bishop, Pavao Zanic, continued to voice his opposition to the Medjugorje happenings. Seeking the Virgin's advice about this matter, the visionaries received this reply: *Fast two days a week for the intentions of the Bishop, who bears a heavy responsibility. If there is a need to, I will ask for a third day. Pray each day for the Bishop.*

In August, Jakov questioned the Virgin concerning orders from the bishop to Father Tomislav Pervan, now the parish priest, to stop the visionaries from saying the rosary and the Lord's Prayer, the Hail Mary, and the Glory Be the customary seven times at the beginning of their time of prayer: *If it is so, then do not go against it so as not to provoke any quarrels. If it is possible, talk about it tomorrow among yourselves. All of you come to an agreement beforehand.*

Later, in the same month, she added, *Pray more for your spiritual life. Do your utmost in this sense. Pray for your Bishop.*

This strong constant in the messages continued: *Pray. When I give you this message, do not be content to just listen to it. Increase your prayer and see how it makes you happy. All graces are at your disposal. All you have to do is to gain them. In order to do that, I tell you—pray!*

In October, the Virgin admonished the visionaries with this message: *My Son suffers very much because men do not want to be reconciled. They have not listened to me. Be converted, be reconciled.*

Later in the same month, she told them, *The important thing is to pray to the Holy Spirit so that He may descend on you. When one has Him, one has everything. People make a mistake when they turn only to the saints to request something. Begin by calling on the Holy Spirit each day. The most important thing is to pray to the Holy Spirit. When the Holy Spirit descends on earth, then everything becomes clear and everything is transformed. I know that many will not believe you, and that many who have an impassioned faith will cool off. You remain firm, and motivate people to instant prayer, penance, and conversion. At the end, you will be happier.*

The mother of Jesus was making it clear that she was there to harvest every possible soul for Him. She appeared determined to stay until that goal was accomplished.

For God so loved the world that he gave his only Son, that whoever believes in him should not perish but have eternal life. For God sent the Son into the world, not to condemn the world, but that the world might be saved through him.—JOHN 3:16-17.

11
The Plan

On direct instructions from the Virgin, Mirjana gave an important synopsis of the apparitions to her spiritual director. What she gave him was a general outline of why the Blessed Virgin Mary had been sent to Medjugorje.

Nearly 18 months of unprecedented daily apparitions had transformed far more than a handful of villagers in central Bosnia-Hercegovina. News of the mystical event was spreading swiftly, and pilgrims were now coming from many parts of the world. Scientists, medical experts, and theologians were constantly present in the village, either performing batteries of tests on the visionaries, or requesting to do so.

More important, the specific plan and purpose of the apparitions was becoming clear through the messages themselves. The synopsis given to Father Vlasic by Mirjana confirmed this plan. Through Mirjana the Virgin then asked the priest to convey this information to the Pope. Here is what

Father Vlasic wrote to Pope John Paul II in December 1983:

During the apparition of December 25, 1982, according to Mirjana, the Madonna confided to her the tenth and last secret, and revealed to her the dates in which the different secrets will be realized. The Blessed Virgin revealed to Mirjana some aspects of the future up to this point in greater detail than to the other seers. For this reason, I am reporting here what Mirjana told me in a conversation of November 5, 1983.

I summarize the essentials of her account, without literal quotation. Mirjana told me that before the visible sign is given to mankind, there will be three warnings to the world. The warnings will be in the form of events on earth. Mirjana will be a witness to them. Ten days before one of the admonitions, Mirjana will notify a priest of her choice. The witness of Mirjana will be a confirmation of the apparitions and a stimulus for the conversion of the world.

After the admonitions, the visible sign will appear on the site of the apparitions in Medjugorje for all the world to see. The sign will be given as a testimony to the apparitions and in order to call people back to faith. The ninth and tenth secrets are serious. They concern chastisement for the sins of the world. Punishment is inevitable, for we cannot expect the whole world to be converted.

The punishment can be diminished by prayer and penance, but it cannot be eliminated. Mirjana says that one of the evils that threatened the world, the one contained in the seventh secret, has been averted thanks to prayer and fasting.[8] That is why the Blessed Virgin continues to encourage prayer and fasting (as she tells us): *You have forgotten that through prayer and fasting you can avert wars and suspend the laws of nature.*

After the first admonition, the others will follow in a rather short time. Thus, people will have some time for conversion. That interval will be a period of grace and conversion. After the visible sign appears, those who are still alive will have little time for conversion.

For that reason, the Blessed Virgin invites us to urgent conversion and reconciliation. The invitation to prayer and penance is meant to avert evil and war, but most of all to save souls. According to Mirjana, the events predicted by the Blessed Virgin are near. By virtue of this experience, Mirjana proclaims to the world: "Convert as quickly as possible. Open your hearts to God."

In addition to this basic message, Mirjana related an apparition she had in 1982, which we believe sheds some light on aspects of Church history. She spoke of an apparition in which Satan appeared to her. Satan asked Mirjana to renounce the Madonna and follow him. That way she could be happy in love and in life. He said that following the Virgin, on the contrary, would only lead to suffering. Mirjana rejected him, and immediately the Virgin gave her the following message, in substance: *Excuse me for this, but you must realize that Satan exists. One day he appeared before the throne of God and asked permission to submit the Church to a period of trial. God gave him permission to try the Church for one century. This century is under the power of the Devil, but when the secrets confided to you come to pass, his power will be destroyed. Even now he is beginning to lose his power and has become aggressive. He is destroying marriages, creating division among priests and is responsible for obsessions and murder. You must protect yourselves against these things through fasting and prayer, especially community prayer. Carry blessed objects with you. Put them in your house, and restore the use of holy water.*

Earlier, in a taped interview, Father Tomislav had made this comment: "The visionaries say that with the realization of the secrets entrusted to them by Our Lady, life in the world will change. Afterwards, men will believe like in ancient times. What will change and how it will change, we don't know, given that they don't want to say anything about the secrets."

Soon after this summation was completed and sent to the Pope, Marija was given this message by the Virgin in response to a question by a priest: *You must warn the bishop very soon, and the Pope, with respect to the urgent and the great importance of the message for all mankind. I have already said many times that the peace of the world is in a state of crisis. Become brothers among yourselves; increase prayer and fasting in order to be saved. I know that many will not believe you, and that many who have an impassioned faith will cool off. You remain firm, and motivate people to instant prayer, penance, and conversion. At the end, you will be happier.*

There could now be little doubt about the urgency of the appearances of the Blessed Virgin Mary in Medjugorje.

For every one who does evil hates the light, and does not come to the light, lest his deeds should be exposed. But he who does what is true comes to the light, that it may be clearly seen that his deeds have been wrought in God. —JOHN 16:20–21.

12

Growing Period

The young people's prayer group, formed at the Blessed Virgin's request through Jelena, was definitely a part of the overall plan of Medjugorje. The members of the group grew in spirit and dedication to the task given to them by the Virgin, serving as an example for people of all ages. Jelena received a steady flow of messages and stated that the Virgin blessed her daily, adding: "When she comes to bless me, light flows from her hands. There is something special that emanates from her."

In May 1983, the Virgin started giving Jelena teachings concerning spiritual life, asking her to write them down so that she could entrust them to the authorities of the Church at a later date. Some of the Franciscans thought that these teachings might be the primary purpose of the locutionists' involvement, especially Jelena's involvement, in the events of Medjugorje. A significant teaching by the Virgin was given to Jelena in November: *Begin by calling on the Holy Spirit each day. The most important thing is to pray to the Holy Spirit. When the Holy Spirit descends on earth, then everything becomes clear and everything is transformed.*

A few days later the Virgin directed Jelena to tell the prayer group, *Pray! I am your mother full of goodness, and Jesus is your great friend. Do not fear anything in His presence. Give Him your heart, from the bottom of your heart. Tell Him your sufferings, thus, you will be invigorated in prayer, with a free heart, in a peace without fear.*

The young people who formed the prayer group experienced a new way of living. Time not spent working and doing family chores was now spent in intense prayer and learning. The group included all of the visionaries and the two locutionists, with Marija being the main one chosen to assist and meet with the prayer group regularly, helping them by means of messages from the Virgin, and through her personal witness.

In late December, the Virgin gave this message to Jelena for the group: *My children, pray! I cannot tell you anything else other than to pray. Know that in your life, there is nothing more important than prayer.*

As though to back up this brief message, the Virgin poured out a long, blunt message on the day after Christmas: *The Mass is the greatest prayer of God. You will never be able to understand its greatness. That is why you must be perfect and humble at Mass, and you should prepare yourselves there. There are many Christians who are no longer faithful, because they do not pray any more. Have them begin again to recite each day, at least, seven Our Father's, seven Hail Mary's, seven Glory Be's, and the Creed, once.*

Once again, the Virgin put forth this simple formula of prayer; but she was not through with this particular lesson, one that would apply especially for the faithful in the West.

She continued: *Above all, abstain from television programs. They represent a great peril for your families. After you have seen them, you cannot pray any more. Give up likewise alcohol, cigarettes, and pleasure of this kind.*

And of course, the "lesson" would not be complete without a request for fasting to go along with the prayer: *The fasting which you are doing in eating fish instead of meat, is not fasting but abstinence. The true fast consists in giving up all our sins, but one must also renounce himself, and make the body participate in it. Monthly confession will be a remedy for the Church in the West. Whole sections of the Church could be cured if the believers would go to confession once a month.*

She followed with this message in February: *Pray, pray! How many persons have followed other beliefs or sects and have abandoned Jesus Christ. They create their own gods; they adore idols. How that hurts me! If they could be converted! Like the unbelievers, they are many! That will change only if you help me with your prayers.*

The messages again emphasized that all of the teachings initiated through the six visionaries and the two locutionists were meant personally for them first, and then for the parish. Eventually, they were for everyone who would listen. This period was an important time of learning in preparation for receiving the throngs of people who would come subsequently on pilgrimage to witness for themselves the grace being poured out in Medjugorje.

In March 1984, the Virgin took the apparitions to another level as she began giving personal weekly messages to the parish on Thursday evenings—as always, through Marija. The teaching was now being expanded to the entire parish, as the Virgin stated in the first of her weekly messages to Marija: *Dear children! I have chosen this parish in a special way and I wish to lead it. I am guarding it in love and I wish everyone to be mine. Thank you for your response this evening. I wish that you will always be here in greater numbers with me and my Son. Every Thursday, I will give a special message to you. Thank you for your response to my call.*

The villagers were happily stunned at such personal attention by the mother of Jesus. For several weeks, the church was filled to overflowing. Many men were also present and remained for longer periods of time, especially when there was Adoration of the Blessed Sacrament. It was a wonderful beginning to the new phase of messages.

March 25 marked another significant milestone in the apparitions. It was the one-thousandth day of continuous apparitions at Medjugorje, a number unprecedented in history. On that day the Virgin gave this startling message: *Rejoice with me and with my angels, because a part of my plan has already been realized. Many have been converted, but many do not want to be converted. Pray!* She then looked at the visionaries for a long time, and tears of happiness flowed down her cheeks. Three days later, in marked contrast, she said, *Many persons come here out of curiosity and not as pilgrims.*

True to humanity, the enthusiasm of receiving such remarkable personal teachings soon waned. The admonition continued as crowds, which only a few weeks before had filled the church, dwindled. How could such a remarkable event be taken for granted so quickly? A personal message to one of the visionaries on April 5 was somber: *If you would be strong in the faith, Satan would not be able to do anything against you. Begin to walk the path of my messages.*

Be converted, be converted, be converted!

In the weekly message for the parish that evening, the Virgin made this plea: *Dear children, this evening I am especially asking you to venerate the heart of my Son, Jesus. Make atonement for the wounds inflicted to the heart of my Son. That heart has been offended with all sorts of sin. Thank you for coming this evening.*

Then, on Thursday, April 26, the Virgin gave no message. The small assembly of faithful villagers gathered in the church were saddened and puzzled; Marija concluded that possibly the Virgin had been giving the weekly message only during Lent.

Several days later, Marija asked her: "Dear Lady, why have you not given me the message for the parish on Thursday?" The Virgin replied: *Even though I had a special message for the parish to awake the faith of every believer, I do not wish to force anyone to anything he doesn't feel or doesn't want. Only a very small number have accepted the messages on Thursdays. At the beginning, there were more, but now it seems as if it has become something ordinary to them. And some have been asking recently for the message only out of curiosity, and not out of faith and devotion to my Son and me.*

Two weeks later, with the church filled once again with those who were convicted by the admonition of the last weekly message, the Virgin said to them in motherly assurance: *I am still speaking to you and I intend to continue. Just listen to my instructions.*

The next two weeks brought further assurance that the Virgin Mary was there personally for everyone who would take the time to listen. On May 17 she said, *Dear children, today I am very happy because there are many who desire to devote themselves to me. I thank you! You have not made a mistake. My son, Jesus Christ, wishes to bestow on you special graces through me. My Son is happy because of your dedication.*

This message was followed on May 24 with these loving words: *I have told you already that I have chosen you in a special way, the way you are. I, the Mother, love you all. And in any moment when it is difficult for you, don't be afraid. I love you even when you are far away from me and my Son. I ask you not to allow my heart to cry with tears of blood because of the souls who are being lost in sin. Therefore, dear children, pray, pray, pray!*

The lessons became more intense as in her July 12 message the Virgin implored all who would listen to her: *These days Satan is trying to thwart all my plans. Pray that his plan may not be fulfilled. I will pray to my Son, Jesus, that He will give you the grace to experience his victory in Satan's temptations.*

The theme remained the same in the following weeks. But from time to time, as the Virgin always seemed to do, she would give a word of encouragement, such as this one on September 13: *Dear children, I continually need your prayer. You wonder what all these prayers are for. Turn around, dear children, and you will see how much ground sin has gained in this world. Therefore, pray that Jesus conquers.*

What greater grace could there be than to have the Blessed Virgin speaking weekly to a community of people and guiding them to live a holy life? These weekly messages were given, of course, in addition to the regular daily messages given to the visionaries. It must be noted again that without the members of the community converting according to the teachings, God's plan for the entire world to have an opportunity to respond in the same manner, would in all probability have failed.

The intensive investigations of the visionaries continued. Every possible type of test was conducted, including the crude and primitive. Needles were stuck into Vicka's arms, and tremendous noise was blasted into Ivan's ears, while they were in ecstasy during the time of apparition. Neither flinched nor sustained any physical damage to their senses. The Franciscans soon put an end to such tests.

Beyond the positive results of the scientific tests, there was a powerful factor far more convincing in the growing acceptance of such a miracle: the ordinariness of the visionaries. That was especially true in the case of little Jakov, only ten years old when the apparitions commenced, and now, three years later, an impetuous 13-year-old boy. Jakov loved to joke and play; but during the apparitions and when being questioned by various authorities, he was well mannered, serious, and straightforward in his answers.

At school, however, Jakov was all boy. One evening during the daily apparition, the Blessed Virgin reproached the young visionary because he had behaved badly toward some of the other boys at school: *You must love them all,* she told him. Jakov then responded that he did love them but that they annoyed him and provoked him. *Then accept it as a sacrifice, and offer it,* she replied, most probably with an understanding, motherly smile.

When the visionaries again questioned the Virgin out of curiosity about how long the apparitions would continue, she answered, *Everything passes exactly according to God's plan. Have patience, persevere in prayer and in penance. Everything happens in its own time.*

These were such simple, but profound teachings. But always, at the core, each message gave its hearers the impetus to ensure that heaven's plan through Medjugorje would be fulfilled.

I have yet many things to say to you, but you cannot bear them now. When the Spirit of truth comes, he will guide you into all the truth; for he will not speak on his own authority, but whatever he hears he will speak, and he will declare to you the things that are to come.—JOHN 16:12-13.

13
The Heart of Medjugorje

In January 1985 the Blessed Virgin Mary gave a message that may be the most important of all the messages she has given at Medjugorje. Given the depth, scope and global impact of her daily apparitions and messages, that is a strong statement. But as one of the millions touched by the spiritual truths of Medjugorje, and as a reporter of the event, I truly believe in its importance. Because of its striking content, this message summarized the very heart and soul of the Medjugorje phenomenon.

This particular message touched on the strong divisions among the different faiths, as well as on the divergent ethnicity comprising the population of Bosnia-Hercegovina. It is this division that served as a constant reason for the lack of daily peace in the region. From her first day of conversation with the visionaries, the Virgin reminded the people urgently of the need for reconciliation. The heart of this message was meant to apply eventually to the entire world, so filled with conflicts involving religion and ethnic origin.

But this message to the world would have no impact if the people to whom the Virgin was coming daily did not heed her words.

It was evident that unless the people acted on the Virgin's constant emphasis on reconciliation, the heavenly plan that was being made known through the Virgin's appearances in the little village, was doomed for tragic failure. And failure came painfully close. In spite of the great graces being poured out for all of the people of the region, a Catholic could question incredulously whether the same grace ought to be given to an Orthodox or to a Muslim.

The impetus for the January 1985 message came from a manifestation of stubborn national pride, a poisonous pride that reached beyond patriotism. The message came in response to a question by a priest of the Catholic faith who had difficulty understanding the healing of an Orthodox child. His difficulty was not so much the healing as with the fact that the child was a gypsy, and of the Orthodox faith. How, he asked the visionaries in obvious disgust and dismay, could the mother of God intercede for the healing of this child of the faith of the despised ethnic enemy, the Serbians?

The question was put to the Virgin by one of the visionaries. She looked at the priest for a long time before answering. It was not a gaze of disgust, as one might imagine in human terms; rather, it was that of a long-suffering mother possessed with endless patience.

This was her response: *Tell this priest, tell everyone, that it is you who are divided on earth. The Muslims and the Orthodox, for the same reason as Catholics, are equal before my Son and me. You are all my children. Certainly, all religions are not equal, but all men are equal before God, as St. Paul says. It does not suffice to belong to the Catholic Church to be saved, but it is necessary to respect the commandments of God in following one's conscience.*

Those who are not Catholics, are no less creatures made in the image of God, and destined to rejoin someday the House of the Father. Salvation is available to everyone, without exception. Only those who refuse God deliberately are condemned. To him who has been given little, little will be asked for. To whoever has been given much, very much will be required. It is God alone, in His infinite justice, who determines the degree of responsibility and pronounces judgment.

Never in the three and a half years of daily messages had the Virgin been so explicit concerning the divisions that existed in the country where God had chosen to send her. Years of tension were coming to a head-on collision with God's truth. Even the trappings of the priesthood could not restrain the nationalistic pride that would question the miraculous healing of a child.

The Woman was speaking words of wisdom to her children. She was giving them the very heart of her reason for coming and staying with them for so long a time. But many continued to struggle in an attempt to rise above the humanity of rabid nationalism and self to become the good spiritual seeds of daily life.

They would soon pay a horrible price for not taking seriously her admonitions for reconciliation and peace.

Why do you call me "Lord, Lord," and not do what I tell you? Every one who comes to me and hears my words and does them, I will show you what he is like: he is like a man building a house, who dug deep, and laid the foundation upon rock; and when a flood arose, the stream broke against that house, and could not shake it, because it had been well built. But he who hears and does not do them is like a man who built a house on the ground without a foundation; against which the stream broke, and immediately it fell, and the ruin of that house was great. —LUKE 6:46–49.

14

More Change

It was a cold, blustery beginning to 1985, yet the hard-core faithful continued coming to Saint James Church for the evening prayers and the apparition. These were not the pilgrims who usually poured into Medjugorje from throughout the world. In the bitter-cold days of early January, they were mainly the villagers accustomed to difficult conditions. Of course, there was no heat in the church, and many were forced to remain outside in the harsh elements. They were comforted with these words of the Blessed Virgin: *I thank the faithful for having come to church in very bad and cold weather.*

The Virgin never failed to thank the people for enduring hardship to respond to her coming. And she always had words of encouragement and warning, as in this message: *My dear children, Satan is strong. He wishes with all his strength to destroy my plans. Pray only, and do not stop doing it. I will also pray to my Son so that all the plans that*

I have begun will be realized. Be patient and persevere in prayer. Do not permit Satan to take away your courage. He works very hard in the world. Be on your guard!

There was more change to come. But it was important for the Virgin to let the people know the dangers, things as small as harsh weather that could threaten to weaken their resolve. She seemed to be willing to mold the villagers personally and intimately so that they would be the prime example of conversion. And she seemed determined to attend to all possible details to ensure that their conversion would continue.

The Virgin went so far as to request that one of the Franciscan priests, Father Slavko Barbaric, who had served as the visionaries' spiritual advisor since July 1984, remain in the parish for a special work: *I wish for Father Slavko to stay here, to guide the life, and to assemble all the news so that when I leave, there will be a complete image of everything that has happened here. I am also praying now for Slavko, and for all those who work in this parish.*

Father Slavko, highly educated and able to communicate in seven languages, would oversee the accurate recording and translation of the messages. He would also make a detailed record of the apparitions, as well as of claimed cures. He would become, in essence, the "caretaker" of Medjugorje's apparitions, a mission he still continues.

Ironically, Father Slavko had not been assigned to the Medjugorje parish, and thus he had to travel daily to and from his parish approximately 25 miles away. But that little penance was representative of why he was the Virgin's choice for such an important task. Father Slavko was involved in every phase of services, usually leading the rosary prayers each evening, mixing the many languages so that all could understand. In addition, Father Slavko would always find time to hear confessions—again in several different languages.

Three more messages given in the early months of 1985 indicate further how closely the Virgin involved herself in the community. To Marija, she said: *For next week, I invite you to say these words: "I love God in everything." With love, one obtains everything. You can receive many things, even the most impossible. The Lord wishes all the parishes to surrender to Him, and I, too, in Him, desire it. Each evening, make your examination of conscience, but only to give thanks in acknowledgment for everything that His love offers us at Medjugorje.*

When asked about the large number of books and articles that had been written about the apparitions, and about the discussions concerning the apparitions that were being held in many parts of the world, she replied: *See, now I am there in each family, in each home! I am everywhere because I love. Do the same. The world lives from love.*

At times during the apparitions, the visionaries were asked to sing songs for the Virgin; she even indicated some to be favorites. Once, after asking them to sing a song three times, she said: *Excuse me for making you repeat, but I wish you to sing with the heart. You must really do everything with the heart.*

Mirjana, no longer receiving daily apparitions, received the following words on March 18, confirming the Virgin's promise to appear to her at least once each year: *Right now, many are greatly seeking money, not only in the parish, but in the whole world. Woe to those who seek to take everything from those who come, and blessed are those from whom they take everything. . . . May the priests help you because I have entrusted to you a heavy burden, and I suffer from your difficulties. . . .*

Again, the Virgin was endearing herself to the villagers as she commented on events within the parish, especially emphasizing the trend of some villagers to concentrate only on profiting from the apparitions.

The apparition on May 7, 1985, marked another major change in the phenomena. Ivanka, the first visionary to have seen the Blessed Virgin, received the word on this day that she would be given the tenth secret, and thus no longer receive daily apparitions.

Like Mirjana, the young woman found this new devastating. As the apparition ended, the other visionaries immediately noticed that Ivanka remained on her knees in an unmoving state. For them, it was a shock to actually see one of their group in the state of ecstasy that occurred during each apparition. They saw her on her knees with eyes focused upwards on the spot where the Virgin was apparently appearing. Ivanka spoke words, but no sounds came forth, and she seemed to be totally at peace.

That evening, the Blessed Virgin appeared to Ivanka at her home for nearly an hour. She came flanked by two angels, compassionately asking her if she had any special requests. Ivanka asked to see her mother again. Within seconds, her mother appeared, hugged her, and told her she was proud of her, and then disappeared. The Virgin then told Ivanka, *My dear child, today is our last meeting, do not be sad. I will return to see you at each anniversary of the first apparition, beginning next year. Dear child, do not think that you have done anything bad, and that this would be the reason why I'm not returning near to you. No, it is not that.*

With all your heart, you have accepted the plans which my Son and I formulated, and you have accomplished everything. No one in the world has had the grace which you, your brothers and sisters have received. Be happy because I am your mother and I love you from the bottom of my heart. Ivanka, thank you for the response to the call of my Son. Thank you for persevering and remaining always with Him as long as He will ask you.

Dear child, tell all your friends that my Son and I are always with them when they call on us. What I have told you during these years on the secrets, do not speak to anyone about them. Go in the peace of God.

Truly, Ivanka had responded well to the tremendous gift of grace of seeing the Blessed Virgin for so long a time. She had deepened spiritually and looked forward to life as a wife and mother. The gift of seeing her human mother again was as special a blessing as it had been the first time in the early days of the apparitions. She withdrew immediately as much as possible from the spotlight trained on the visionaries and concentrated on living her new life.

Now there were only four visionaries receiving daily apparitions; Jelena and Marijana were still receiving inner visions and locutions. Mirjana received occasional apparitions, as the Virgin had said she would "in time of need," when the weight of the secrets and the ongoing charisma would become too much for her to bear. The Virgin would appear then to comfort her and sometimes give her messages.

Mirjana had a special role. She was the one visionary selected to reveal the ten secrets at the appointed time, through a priest of her choosing. Mirjana chose a priest far from the parish; when questioned about her choice, she responded that "Gospa will take care of it." Shortly thereafter, Father Petar Ljubicic, whom Mirjana had chosen, was transferred to the parish in a move completely unrelated to his being Mirjana's choice.

In the latter part of 1985, the Virgin gave a series of messages pertaining directly to unbelievers, beginning with these words spoken to Mirjana: *My angel, pray for unbelievers. People will tear their hair, brothers will plead with brothers, they will curse their past lives lived without God. They will repent, but it will be too late. Now is the time for conversion. I have been exhorting you for the past four years. Pray for them. Invite everyone to pray the rosary.*

Another message containing this warning: *Those who say, "I do not believe in God," how difficult it will be for them when they will approach the throne of God and hear the voice: "Enter into Hell."*

Yet another message revealed the burden that the Blessed Virgin bears for unbelievers: *They are my children. I suffer because of them. They do not know what awaits them. You must pray more for them.*

Such a string of messages concerning those who deliberately turn away from God shows again the Mother's love for all the children of the world. As she said so many times, she would be there for all, to the very last second of life. Even for the believer who stumbles and gives in to temptation, she had these reassuring words: *With respect to sin, it suffices to give it serious consideration, and soon, move ahead and correct the sin.* In short, we are to contritely ask forgiveness from God, forgive ourselves, and then get on with life.

The Virgin once again showed Mirjana the first of the ten secrets, this time in a vision. Mirjana later described the experience as "like watching a movie." Mirjana recalled seeing a place of desolation as the Virgin said: *It is the upheaval of a region of the world. In the world, there are so many sins. What can I do, if you do not help me? Remember that I love you. God does not have a hard heart. Look around you and see what men do, then you will no longer say that God has a hard heart. How many people come to church, to the house of God, with respect, a strong faith, and love*

God? Very few! Here you have a time of grace and conversion. It is necessary to use it well.

Such messages, accompanied by a vision of their content, were greatly disturbing to the visionaries. But following a word of warning there would usually be a word of comfort, such as this one: *Have you forgotten that you are in my hands?*

And Mary said, "My soul magnifies the Lord, and my spirit rejoices in God my Savior, for he has regarded the low estate of his handmaiden. For behold, henceforth all generations will call me blessed; for he who is mighty has done great things for me, and holy is his name." —LUKE 1:46–49.

15
A Time of Mercy

Mirjana's active role in the apparitions was revived unexpectedly in early 1986, startling both the priests and the pilgrims. However, since she was the visionary appointed to select a priest to reveal each secret as it was about to occur, she herself was not surprised when at this time she began receiving a series of messages by inner locution as well as some apparitions. The Virgin Mary would appear or speak to her interiorly on the second day of each month, concerning the secrets and the preparations for their occurrence.

Was this, as many followers thought, an indication that the apparitions might be coming to an end and that the secrets were soon to be fulfilled? Such speculation came from the knowledge that Mirjana had been appointed to reveal, through a priest of her choosing, the time that the secrets would occur.

No, Mirjana stated, this was not the end of the apparitions. It was, rather, a time of mercy, a period of extra grace.

Even after more than four years of extraordinary messages, the Queen of Peace, as the Virgin made herself known, continued to exhort her children to live the gospel message of her Son.

Along with the series of messages given to Mirjana on the second day of each month, the Virgin continued to give Marija personal, intimate messages for the people of the parish every Thursday evening. Both of these series of messages were, of course, in addition to the messages given during the Virgin's daily appearances to Marija, Vicka, Jakov, and Ivan.

Medjugorje's apparitions, in form so much like those of Fatima, were nonetheless different from the Fatima apparitions mainly because of their daily occurrence, their longevity, and the number of visionaries and locutionists involved. The unusual revival of Mirjana's role concerning the secrets added another dimension of difference. In retrospect, the events of Medjugoje could be seen as merciful guidance from heaven for a world plunging headlong toward separating itself from God's moral law and replacing it with man-made civil law. With the new developments that began in 1986, it seemed as if the Virgin Mary were pleading before the throne of God for just a little more time to reach all her children.

Here is a sampling of the personal messages the Virgin Mary gave to the parish each Thursday evening in 1986:

JANUARY 23—*Today, I invite all of you to pray in order that God's plan with you and all that God wills through you may be realized. Help others to be converted, especially those who are coming to Medjugorje. Dear children, do not allow Satan to reign in your hearts. Do not be an image of Satan, but be my image. I am calling you to pray so that you may be witnesses of my presence. God cannot fulfill His will without you. God gave everyone free will and it is up to you to be disposed.*

FEBRUARY 7—*This parish is elected by me and is special. It is different from others and I am giving great graces to all who are praying from their hearts. Dear children, I am giving you my messages first of all for the parish and then for all others. The messages are first of all for you, and then for others who will accept them. You will be responsible to me and to my Son, Jesus.*

JUNE 5—*I am calling you to decide if you wish to live the messages I am giving you. I wish you to be active in living and transmitting the messages. Especially, dear children, I desire you to be the reflections of Jesus who enlightens an unfaithful world which is walking in darkness. I wish that all of you may be a light to all and witness to the light. Dear children, you are not called to darkness, you are called to light and to live the light in your lives.*

As if to confirm once more that the time of mercy was still active, the Virgin gave this message just before the celebration of the fifth anniversary on June 25: *In these days, the Lord has allowed me to intercede for more graces for you. Therefore, dear children, I want to urge you once again to prayer. Pray constantly and in this way, I will give you the joy which the Lord gives me. With these graces, dear children, I want your suffering to be for you a joy. I am your mother, and I want to help you.*

Late in the night of June 25, the Virgin gave a beautiful message to Ivan and Marija, a message that was later read to nearly one thousand pilgrims gathered on Podbrdo Hill: *You are on a Thabor.*[9] *You receive blessings, strength and love. Carry them into your families and into your homes. To each one of you, I grant a special blessing. Continue in joy, prayer and reconciliation.*

This particular late-night message was important for this writer personally because I was present when it was given during my first pilgrimage to Medjugorje. I vividly remember groping my way up Podbrdo Hill that night, joining a steady stream of pilgrims. No flashlights were allowed because the Communists had banned public gatherings on the hill. It was so dark, I could hardly see the silhouette of the person directly in front of me. I huddled among the rocks in pitch darkness with thousands of other pilgrims, listening to these words from the Blessed Mother.

The main thrust of the message that night was to pray with our families so that the Virgin could present us as *A beautiful flower that unfolds for [her] Son, Jesus. . . .*

Another message of mercy was given on August 4: *Read each Thursday the Gospel of Matthew, where it is said: "No one can serve two masters. . . . You cannot serve God and money."*

Later, the admonition to read this passage of Scripture each Thursday would translate into asking families to read it at least once a week—not just during the Virgin's time of coming to Medjugorje, but as a regular reminder that all is in God's hands.

The time of mercy expanded as in January 1987 the Virgin introduced yet another change in the format of giving the messages: *Dear children! I want to thank you for every response to my call. I want to thank you for all the suffering and prayers you have offered to me. Dear children, I want to give you messages from now onwards no longer every Thursday, but on the 25th of each month. The time has come when what our Lord wanted has been fulfilled. From*

*now on, I give you less messages but I will be with you. There-
fore, dear children, I beg you to listen and to live my messages
so I can guide you.*

Again, the change was interpreted as a sign that the
apparitions were winding down. Any day now, it was
thought by many followers, the Virgin would make her last
appearance and give her final message. But the visionaries
assured the public that no such notice was being given to
them; this change was simply another extension of grace.

Thus, on January 25, 1987, the Blessed Virgin began giving the new monthly messages through Marija,[10] who would
be the only one of the six to receive these special messages.
From her comments and from the wording of the messages,
it was evident that they were meant for publication so that
they could reach everyone.

On the twenty-fifth of each month, immediately following the apparition, Marija would write down the message
and give it to Father Slavko Barbaric. It would then be
checked thoroughly for adherence to Scripture and church
doctrine, and in less than 24 hours, it would be transmitted
to prayer groups and to others around the world.

Other changes were taking place at a dizzying pace. The
streets, fields, and homes of the villagers were now constantly
filled with pilgrims from every corner of the world. The
Communist authorities, finally realizing that their fears of
insurrection were unfounded, began to change tactics. Now
they were beginning to see Medjugorje as a new source of
tourist income. The Virgin Mary was referred to sarcastical-
ly as "Our Lady of Currency." A new form of harassment
commenced as the Communist officials attempted to stop
pilgrims from staying in individual homes and force them to
stay in new, hastily built government accommodations.

But by this time, the flow of pilgrims was too large. The additional rooms constantly being added to the homes of villagers stayed filled in spite of newly passed tax laws that demanded up to 65 percent of the income derived from private accommodations.

The harvest was now reaching far beyond the hills of Medjugorje.

No one can serve two masters; for either he will hate the one and love the other, or he will be devoted to the one and despise the other. You cannot serve God and mammon. Therefore I tell you, do not be anxious about your life, what you shall eat or what you shall drink, nor about your body, what you shall put on. Is not life more than food and the body more than clothing? Look at the birds of the air; they neither sow nor reap nor gather into barns, and yet your heavenly Father feeds them. Are you not of more value than they? And which of you by being anxious can add one cubit to his span of life? And why are you anxious about clothing? Consider the lilies of the field, how they grow; they neither toil nor spin; yet I tell you, even Solomon in all his glory was not arrayed like one of these. But if God so clothes the grass of the field, which today is alive and tomorrow is thrown into the oven, will he not much more clothe you, O men of little faith? Therefore, do not be anxious, saying "What shall we eat?" or "What shall we wear?" For the Gentiles seek all these things; and your heavenly Father knows that you need them all. But seek first his kingdom and his righteousness, and all these things shall be yours as well. Therefore, do not be anxious about tomorrow, for tomorrow will be anxious for itself. Let the day's own trouble be sufficient for the day. —MATTHEW 6:24–34.

PART III

Fruits

So, every sound tree bears good fruit, but the bad tree bears evil fruit. A sound tree cannot bear evil fruit, nor can a bad tree bear good fruit. Every tree that does not bear good fruit is cut down and thrown into the fire. Thus you will know them by their fruits.

—MATTHEW 7:17–20.

16
The Call

The apparitions had now developed into a major force for spiritual conversion, with their story reaching millions of people. In October 1985 it reached me. Two years later, I sat in the coolness of the shady side of Saint James Church in Medjugorje, shaking my head in wonder that shortly, I would be standing at the altar giving a talk to the English-speaking pilgrims.

My life had changed dramatically since I first heard about the apparitions. Though I had felt "The Call" from God in the past, this was my first attempt to truly respond. God's call had come through a source totally foreign to me, the apparitions of the Blessed Virgin Mary, a woman of Scripture to whom I had paid little attention.

No longer was success in business my prime motivation. Now my focus was on spreading the message of Medjugorje, a message of renewal and hope, a reiteration of the Gospel message. I was now immersed in a busy schedule of national and international travel, telling the story of the apparitions and giving witness of what The Call had done in my life.

In the brief space of 20 months, I had traveled to Medjugorje four times. I had spend many hours in Saint James Church listening to priestly homilies and talks by others who were inspired by the dramatic spiritual changes brought about by the daily apparitions. Now, I would be the one to stand and speak.

I gave my witness only as further evidence of the conversion process that transpires when the heart is moved by the presence of the Blessed Virgin Mary. In retrospect, I would not now be writing my fourth book about this phenomenon, or still traveling the world to spread its messages, if the personal events I related in my talk that afternoon had not occurred.

Here are excerpts from my story as I gave it that afternoon:

During the past fifteen months, I have given many talks on the Blessed Virgin Mary's apparitions in Medjugorje and my personal conversion as a result. But here in Medjugorje, I am a pilgrim the same as everyone else. Never in my deepest thoughts would I have envisioned one day standing here speaking to you, my fellow pilgrims.

I am a Lutheran by faith. One Sunday in October 1985, in our Sunday school class we were talking about modern day miracles. At the end of the session, someone mentioned what was occurring here in Medjugorje. As a newspaper journalist, my interest immediately turned to what a good article it would be for my newspapers. That was the extent of my interest in Medjugorje, just to write one article about it.

After class, I asked the lady who had told us about Medjugorje if she had more information on the apparitions. She told me she had a Catholic friend who had first told her about Medjugorje, and that she had a small book and a recently made videotape that actually showed the young visionaries during the time of an apparition. I knew virtually nothing about past apparitions, such as those that reportedly took place at Fatima or Lourdes. And I knew nothing about the Catholic Church or the Blessed Virgin Mary. The only thing I knew about her is what is in the Bible in the Gospel of Luke.

I read the small book on the apparitions first and was impressed with what was happening here. I could not understand why I had not heard about it sooner. Still, it did not touch me spiritually. Several evenings later, my wife Terri and I watched the videotape. As soon as the tape began, I knew in my heart that Medjugorje's apparitions were real.

Journalists do not go by "feelings." We have to have hard, cold facts on a subject, and then we are to report it as objectively as possible. Suddenly, as I watched the tape, there was no objectivity, only an inner knowledge that it was real. It is still difficult for me to explain that about halfway through the viewing of that videotape, I suddenly felt a message within my heart. The message was from the Virgin Mary and she said to me, *You are my son, and I am asking you to do my Son's will.*

She asked me to write about the apparitions of Medjugorje, and if I said yes, the spreading of the messages would become my life's mission. I was so startled that I looked around to see where the voice was coming from. There was no doubt the Blessed Virgin was speaking to me, but my humanity and my professional training kept saying this was impossible.

I looked at Terri; she had not moved. When the video was over, I tried to tell her what had happened to me. She looked at me for a long time, then said I was probably just overwhelmed with what I had seen. Terri went to bed after we talked a while and then I watched the tape again. Afterwards, I fell to my knees, and for the first time in my life, I truly prayed from the depths of my soul.

I kept asking, why me? And why would she be speaking to a Protestant? I knew I was not worthy. That was not due to modesty; rather, what my life had been to this point. I was in the chase for the American success story, making lots of money, having prestige, and enjoying the fruits of my labor. That was the center of my life. Although I was active in my Lutheran church, serving on the church council and teaching a Sunday school class, the truth was that I had no real spirituality. I had never attempted to answer the call from God. My prayers were limited to time at church. Now I was praying as never before, on my living room floor.

The next morning, the message was still in my heart. I went to my office and attempted to write about what I had been through in the past 24 hours, but nothing seemed to come out right. I felt another message at that time, gently admonishing me to pray and study more. So, for the next five weeks, I read everything I could get my hands on about Medjugorje; I read about Lourdes and Fatima and other past apparitions.

Then I started writing, and it just poured forth from the heart. Still, I tried to be objective. One column would never tell the entire story, so I decided to do a four-part series, which ran in December 1985. The public reaction was very positive, even though our region is predominantly Protestant. Catholics, Protestants, everyone reacted favorably. It was evident there was a great spiritual hunger and curiosity as to what this was all about. People immediately began writing and telephoning, asking for copies of the articles.

In May 1986 I made my first trip to Medjugorje. I did not come seeking proof of the apparitions; but rather to bask in the spirituality, this love of God that is so prevalent here. It seemed as if every time I turned around, there was another spiritual lightning bolt. The people, the priests, they were all part of it. I didn't eat or sleep much. I wanted to enjoy every waking moment.

I'll never forget the day I had to return home. I came here to Saint James Church at six o'clock in the morning and knelt in the front pew praying to God for the strength to be able to take this home and do something with it. The truth was, I didn't want to leave. After the Mass, I went behind the church and cried like a little child.

Only now am I beginning to understand. When we come here, we have to become as a child. We have to open our heart and soul and be a child of Mary. We have to give everything to Jesus. I feel I began doing just that on the last morning of that first pilgrimage. When Terri met me at the airport on my return home, I was too filled with emotion to even speak. I could only cry. We went home and sat for several hours. Finally, I started telling her about my experience.

The next morning, Sunday, we went to our Lutheran church and everyone kept asking me about Medjugorje. I would just look at them and my eyes would fill with tears. I just wanted to return home. It would take many days to adjust to being "earth-bound" again, because the trip to Medjugorje had been like a touch of heaven, and I wanted to feel it forever.

I knew I had been given a mission but no real idea of its depth. In September 1986 I finally convinced Terri she needed to make a pilgrimage, because I knew we would both be involved in spreading this message. We have two small children, and Terri did not want to leave the children to come to Medjugorje. She said she believed and did not need to go. I told her yes, she did, because I knew that in her heart our children came first, even before God. She had to come and find out her first priority.

Even as I took her to the airport, she was trying to get out of coming. But when she returned home, she quietly told me that while in Medjugorje, she temporarily "forgot" her children, didn't think about them very much, and didn't think about home. It was a very important pilgrimage because without her support and belief, there would be very little I could do to accomplish what the Virgin Mary was asking of me. We realized that this was a mission for the entire family.

Those of us who come to Medjugorje today find it different from what it was in the beginning, or what we have read about. It is more commercial now, and a little more difficult to find real peace. That was inevitable. It is a minor miracle that it is not worse. The holiness and spirituality are here if we seek it. I am but one person who was given something to do by God. I struggled with it. Now, I don't. I just listen and try to do what Jesus is instructing us to do through His mother.

Sometimes it is necessary to simply go off some place quiet and not really say anything. Just sit in the presence of God and let Him speak. That is what we are to take home from Medjugorje. Not the phenomenon itself; not the miracle of the spinning sun, or other wonders, or getting into the apparition room.

The room in the rectory where the visionaries go each evening for the time of the apparition is very plain and undistinguished. It is just like Medjugorje. Actually it serves as a bedroom and an office for one of the priests. But during the time of the evening apparition, it is one of the holiest spots in the world. It is a place where God pours out His love. That is what we have to do with our Medjugorje experience, to put an encasement of love around it and make it holy. What takes place in this church and what takes place in our hearts, that is the real purpose of the apparitions at Medjugorje.

Look at the villagers and your fellow pilgrims. Look into their eyes and you will see what the message is really about. It is pure love. It is about being able to share and giving of self, regardless of the consequences. These villagers live under a Communist government, which oppresses them because of their faith. These simple, hard-working people give up so much to live their faith. Compare them with our lives, our churches, where we are free to live and to worship. We give so little in comparison.

Not being able to take communion at Mass causes me to die a little each time because I want to receive Jesus in the Eucharist so much. It is for that reason I desire to some day convert to Catholicism. I see many Catholics receive the Eucharist where it seems to mean little to them. I want to say to them, "Do you understand that the miracle that takes place on this altar when bread and wine are transformed into the very flesh and blood of Jesus, is a far greater miracle than the apparitions that take place here in Medjugorje?"

I could remain a Lutheran and live this message and be close to Jesus and Mary. When I am invited to give talks, it isn't just Catholics who attend; it is also many Protestants, Muslims, Jews, and others. They are listening, because Medjugorje is a holy miracle not meant for people of just one faith, but for every living being.

The Blessed Virgin Mary put it this way in one of her

messages when asked about the different faiths: *My Son and I do not cut the cake where faiths are concerned. You have put the walls, the division between yourselves. . . .*

Our Lady went on to say that Jesus looks into our hearts for love. Once, when the visionaries were asking about the many faiths, Mary told them that there was a woman who was a neighbor to one of the visionaries (Mirjana, in her home city of Sarajevo), who was a great example of holiness. The visionaries looked at her in shock and asked how that could be since this woman was Muslim. Mary answered that was for God to decide, not for us; that we should first take care of ourselves spiritually. It is not our job to judge others because of their beliefs. It is our job to help change our families, our communities, our entire country through prayer, through living this message of love and peace.

How often she has come in apparition here asking us to seek peace, and to pray, fast, do penance. The full power of prayer is still unknown to many. The rosary, this little string of beads of which many Protestants are unfamiliar, this is what she is asking us to pray. To pray it daily and with our families. This is a powerful prayer! She said so in her apparitions at Fatima and Lourdes, and she has said so here in Medjugorje. It is a prayer focusing on the major mysteries, life, and Scripture references of Jesus. And it is not just meant for Catholics.

I gave a talk in New Orleans several months ago, and on the last stop of the tour I was to speak in a small Lutheran church. All week the people who had brought me to New Orleans kept saying not to expect too much at the Lutheran church. It was a new church that held only two hundred people. And whatever I did, they said, don't mention the rosary! They did not want to upset our Protestant brothers and sisters.

We drove to the little Lutheran church that evening and the parking lot was overflowing with cars. I thought, well, at least we will have a good crowd. On entering, we found close to four hundred people squeezed into that church!

Frankly, I never know what I am going to say when I speak, because I do not prepare or use notes. I just pray to the Holy Spirit and give what comes from within. About halfway through my talk, something wonderful happened. I suddenly held up the rosary and said to them, "I've just got to tell you about the rosary!"

In attendance was a young Catholic woman who had brought approximately a hundred rosaries to the talk in hopes that she could give them to the Lutherans. She had asked me to mention that she had them, so as I began to talk about the rosary, I mentioned that this woman had brought rosaries to give to anyone who wanted one. Two minutes after my talk, the rosaries were gone!

The divisions that we place between us as Catholics and non-Catholics, as Muslim and Jew, are divisions we have created. And, we don't need them. All we need is the love and effort through faith in God to understand and listen to each other. How much we would accomplish if only we did that.

Even here in Medjugorje, one sees divisions among the people. We see arguments, pushing and shoving among the pilgrims. It is hard to understand that people come here for holiness and yet, sometimes it is like we are in a bargain basement looking for discounts. Our Lady reminds us constantly to be at peace through forgiveness and reconciliation, and to seek it here by praying.

The villagers are strained with all that has transpired here. Six years of constant guests in their homes, the church packed all the time with no seats available to them. People all over their fields and all through their village. We have disrupted their lives; yet, for six years, they have prayed for us. I ask now that we pray for them. Because everywhere Mary goes, Satan goes also; and he is very busy here. The youth of the village are tempted with the growing number of bars and nightclubs. One even hears rock and roll music on the hill where Mary first appeared. Commercialism is rampant. How do we find peace amongst all of this, developing in parallel with the search for holiness?

We need to pray for these people, pray for tolerance for them, and that the temptation of greed and materialism is abated. This is a holy place, and I would say that a majority of the villagers are exactly what you have read about or seen in videos about Medjugorje. But they suffer the temptations of the world just as we do, even with the apparition taking place daily.

There is a special volume of books called *The Poem of the Man-God* that has just been translated into English from the original Italian, written by an Italian mystic, Maria Valtorta. There is a story in volume one that I feel describes why the Blessed Virgin Mary is the one chosen to bring us these messages.

It begins with Jesus in a small village preparing to speak. There is such a great crowd of people that he is asked to climb to the top of a balcony on the side of the owner's house to give His talk. Mary is there with Him as she was much of the time of His ministry. She joins Him on the balcony, sitting on the next step down from where He is standing.

After the talk, Jesus as usual begins to perform healings. Suddenly, a young mother comes forward from the crowd, pleading to Him in a loud voice. She has a ten-year-old son in her arms who is paralyzed, and she cries out, "Jesus, Jesus, please heal my son! He fell from this very balcony where You are!"

The elders and Pharisees of the village look at Jesus to see what He will do. Jesus asks her to bring her son up the stairs of the balcony. As she starts up, she stumbles in her excitement, and Mary immediately goes to her saying, "Here, give him to me. I am a mother also and I understand."

Mary takes the little boy to Jesus who places His hands on him and says, "Be happy!"

The little boy squirms out of Mary's embrace, begins to cry, and runs to his mother. It takes the crowd a few seconds to realize that the little boy has been healed. The elders and Pharisees then turn to Jesus and say, "Always in the past when you healed someone, you would say 'go and sin no more,' or 'your sins are forgiven.' But with this little boy, you did not do that. Why?"

Jesus looks at His questioners, smiles, and says, "The little boy was in my mother's arms. That was all that was necessary!"

Mary is the greatest human example of spiritual love. She is the spiritual mother of all of God's children. Mary has had her arms around me since I first timidly began to attempt to answer my own calling. She places her arms around each one of us, and she brings each one of us here to give us this precious gift of God's love.

That is the purpose and the message of Medjugorje.

As usual, I had not prepared anything special for the talk; I had simply prayed to the Holy Spirit to allow me to say whatever was needed for the group assembled there. At the end, I was greeted with warm applause. Unbeknownst to me, the priest in charge that afternoon had taped the talk and presented me a copy to take home to my wife. Later, I discovered that two women, one from Ireland and one from

Scotland, had also asked for and received a copy of the tape.

Within less than a year, thousands of copies of the tape had been distributed all over Ireland and the United Kingdom, with the proceeds being used to send priests to Medjugorje. That tape would help pave the way for my mission far beyond the borders of the United States.

John said to him, "Teacher, we saw a man casting out demons in your name, and we forbade him, because he was not following us." But Jesus said, "Do not forbid him; for no one who does a mighty work in my name will be able soon after to speak evil of me." —MARK 9:38–41.

17
Sons and Daughters

As the fifth anniversary of the apparitions arrived, on June 25, 1986, everything seemed to be going according to heaven's plan. And while the villagers had adjusted to the dramatic changes created by the Virgin's appearances among them, most aspects of daily life continued as they had before the apparitions.

Even the lives of the visionaries, open to constant public scrutiny, followed traditional patterns. Ivanka was now married and was the mother of a little girl. She had slipped quietly into the background of village life, and was disturbed only briefly when she announced plans to marry her childhood friend Reyko Elez in June. How, the villagers and pilgrims alike asked, could she marry, when the Virgin had recommended that the visionaries adopt a holy life as priests and nuns?

Ivanka was quick to answer. Yes, the Blessed Virgin did say it would be good if they pursued a religious vocation, but she also said she would honor whatever course they chose; and, she added, somewhat testily, "Marriage is also a sacrament of the Church!"

For Ivan, life in the village was interrupted by a required one-year tour of military service. During his short period of adjustment to military life, the Virgin did not appear to him in apparition; instead, she spoke to him via inner locution. Only after he was settled into this new way of life did she begin reappearing in locations away from the barracks where he was stationed. On completion of his military duty, the shy, introverted Ivan returned to the village, more mature, and possessing a new confidence that became evident in his dealings with pilgrims. He now met frequently with pilgrim groups and answered their questions with calm patience.

Mirjana had returned to Sarajevo for university studies, while Marija and Vicka took on the never-ending task of meeting with the increasing crowds of pilgrims. The two young women would spend long hours each day meeting patiently with groups, answering the same questions repeatedly, and praying over the sick and handicapped. True to form, Jakov stayed away from the pilgrims except for appearances in the apparition room each evening. His days were filled with the carefree ways of a teenage boy.

Away from Saint James Church, new buildings dotted the landscape. Commercialism grew at a rampant pace, and taxis roamed like a swarm of bees over decrepit bridges and dirt roads that were never intended to support such traffic. The roads were filled with pilgrims, and many villagers were busy adding extensions of rooms to their dwellings to house more pilgrims. For many villagers, the changes were uncomfortable annoyances, offset only by the good fruits of the apparitions.

But more ominous changes were taking place on the world scene, changes that would have a different effect on the region where the Virgin had appeared daily now for five years. From the first day of speaking to the visionaries, she had issued urgent warnings for the people to reconcile, pray, and fast. For the most part, prayer and fasting became part of the daily life. On Fridays, the popular day for fasting, it was all but impossible to get any type of meal that included meat in the restaurants, snack booths, and homes where pilgrims stayed.

Still, the call for reconciliation was largely ignored. Croat, Serb, and Muslim refused to forget a lifetime of learning to hate one another. Out of such obstinacy, the seeds of war began to take root.

As the fifth anniversary of the apparitions was celebrated, Communism, the dragon of evil that for more than 70 years had ruled a vast part of Eastern Europe, inexplicably began to crumble under the weight of the increasing demands of freedom-hungry people. As Communism toppled, many countries found themselves in a state of political and social turmoil. Divisive wars within newly freed countries, especially those of the former Soviet Union, raged for the prize of controlling power. Religious and ethnic persecution quickly reached new heights as ultranationalism spread.

The demise of the dragon of Communism originated in Poland and quickly spread into neighboring countries. The people of the nations making up the Federation of Yugoslavia, oppressed ruthlessly and dominated by staunch Communists for more than forty years, finally saw a faint light of hope for true freedom. Many in Croatia and Bosnia-Hercegovina mistakenly viewed the apparitions only as a sign that at last, God had come to set them free from the political chains of oppression. This assumption was a mistake: The Yugoslav oppressors, dominated by Serbians, began making plans to maintain power.

With a pronounced sense of urgency, the Virgin's messages continued to appeal for her children to listen carefully and carry out her lessons. She knew what was about to happen if true conversion and reconciliation did not take place in the hearts of the people.

By the spring of 1988, I was well into the mission of spreading the Medjugorje message—thanks in part to the widespread distribution of the tape of my 1987 talk in Saint James Church. Just as in Bosnia-Hercegovina, for the majority of those I encountered the road to conversion needed to begin with reconciliation. So many lives had been shattered because of divisions. So many marriages had been broken by divorce, leaving children without the security of family. So many divisions existed among Christians, spawned often by petty disagreements and maintained out of pride. Division was clearly Satan's tool of choice.

The mission to which I had been called was now international, allowing me to visit a country I had long admired and desired to see, Ireland. During an earlier tour there, I had been through nearly every Irish county, except for the six counties comprising Northern Ireland. Now, I was to make a second tour during which I would see firsthand why the Blessed Virgin pleads so urgently for reconciliation among her children. This time, I would visit Northern Ireland.

For hundreds of years, Catholics and Protestants have waged a murderous war against each other in the north of Ireland. Many Americans think that all of Ireland is directly involved, but in fact the conflict is concentrated in only a small section of six northern counties. Division comes from the fact that the predominantly Protestant people of these counties are attached politically to the United Kingdom of

Great Britain and Northern Ireland. That status is an unacceptable sore point with the predominantly Catholic people of the remaining Irish counties, which make up the Republic of Ireland.

The Irish Catholics demand that all of Ireland be part of the Republic of Ireland, while the Protestants of the northern counties cling stubbornly to their kinship with the British. In this state of tension lies the heart of the problem. But the cause of the problem is no longer its impetus: After generations of feuding between the two opposing sides, the conflict has taken on a life of its own. Terrorist war continues, fueled by hatred spawned by the latest atrocities from each side.

In my first talk in Northern Ireland on the apparitions of Medjugorje, I asked how many in attendance were Protestant. I did so because I had been told that many Protestants would come. Not one hand went up.

Embarrassed, I wondered why I had asked such a stupid question, but went on with the talk. I attempted to plant the message of Medjugorje in the hearts of all present, hoping to bring a ray of hope to a seemingly hopeless situation. I told them that Medjugorje's message is a message of love and peace, not war—especially war among people who claim to be Christians.

After the talk, many in attendance approached me with a variety of comments and questions. I was shocked when one of them told me in a hushed, serious tone that there were many Protestants present at the talk, but that they had not revealed themselves out of fear. I further discovered that in daily life in Northern Ireland, many Catholics and Protestants live and work together side by side. It is the militant, fanatical Catholic and Protestant groups, formed into armies of hatred and identified by nationalistic names or initials, who continue the senseless slaughter.

For historical reasons, the Virgin Mary is considered by many Protestants to be only for Catholics. Protestants often do not accept her role as spiritual mother and messenger for our Lord. But I told the audiences that her Medjugorje message is not just Catholic or even just Christian. It is a pure message of love, a unifying love—a unifying, forgiving love, a reaffirmation of prophecies of the Old Testament as well as of the gospel message of Christ.

During my remaining talks on the tour, I told audiences that the Blessed Virgin always begins her messages with the opening words, "Dear Children." I reminded them that she is not speaking just to the six visionaries of Medjugorje. She is addressing her words to all of her children who will listen. That number includes both her Protestant and Catholic sons and daughters.

What has been given to us at Medjugorje, I reiterated throughout the tour, is that every daughter and every son of every family and every faith, is a spiritual child of Mary, who has been given the motherly task of leading us to God. She was given this task at the foot of the cross as Jesus gave the ultimate gift of redemptive suffering, and said to His mother: "Woman, behold your son!" And then to His disciple John, who was standing in for all of us, He said: "Behold your mother!"

I used this dramatic scriptural moment, uttered from the depths of despair and unimaginable human suffering, to define Mary's role as a human spiritual mother for all of us, as appointed by God. She is not a goddess who takes the place of Jesus; she is a mother who lovingly invites everyone to come to her Son. She has been sent by God in supernatural apparition time and again throughout the ages to ensure that the gift of redemptive suffering is not sacrificed in vain.

The Blessed Virgin calls for prayer because of the sorry

condition of the world, and, I stressed to my Irish audiences, the division of Ireland is a stark example of that shameful condition. Just as is true of the fractricidal struggle among the people of the former Federation of Yugoslavia, the centuries-old struggle between Irish Catholic and Irish Protestant is a painful example of the sorry human condition that God desires to heal by sending the mother of Jesus to earth.

Yet, there is a burning spiritual hunger in Ireland and throughout the world. Everywhere I traveled in that beautiful country, I saw that hunger, and I heard it from the people. People want to be good. They want God in their lives. I reminded the crowds gathered at each conference in Ireland that they are part of that spiritual hunger. Over and over during those first seven years of her apparitions at Medjugorje, I told my audiences, she said to the visionaries, *I come because I want you to be in Heaven with My Son, Jesus.*

I related how in Medjugorje I observed Protestants and Catholics, Muslims and Jews, unbelievers and agnostics, skeptics and outright opponents, coming there on pilgrimage. And I watched as many of them experienced a dazzling conversion through the peace and love of the event as it unfolded for them. How wonderful it was to see those of the Jewish faith come to Medjugorje. Some would convert to Christianity; others would return home more devout in their Jewish faith. The same was true of many non-believers, Muslims, and Protestants.

Thus, the overriding message that God laid on my heart to give to the Irish on this tour was that we must learn to love our brothers and sisters, not with talk, but by actually doing what God asks us to do. We can do what God asks if we listen to and then apply the messages of Medjugorje to our daily life. We can apply the message to the very smallest things, such as smiling and saying thank you to people, and really meaning it. And we can apply the message to larger issues such as accepting circumstances that cross our wills, and giving generously of our material gifts to those in need—gifts that come from God in the first place.

I pointed out that if the apparitions were actually Satan disguised as the Blessed Virgin Mary—a fear expressed by many people from other faiths, it was the worst mistake he had ever made! Satan certainly cannot go up against himself, as stated in Scripture. He cannot lead millions of people to God. And yet, millions of people have come to God through the message of Medjugorje.

I often told my audiences of the time several years ago when I took a Baptist minister and a Lutheran pastor to Medjugorje. I was surprised that the Baptist minister had little difficulty accepting Mary's presence as a messenger of God. His only difficulty lay, of course, in the interpretation of Scripture from the Baptist perspective. He was able, however, to see the beauty and the goodness that was coming from Medjugorje. He was a direct witness to the good fruits of conversion to God.

The Lutheran pastor, on the other hand, returned home after his pilgrimage, completely confused and dismayed. He had thought of Medjugorje only in ecumenical terms. For him, the Medjugorje phenomenon was the coming together of the people of all faiths, and to him, coming together meant sharing the sacraments, especially the holy Eucharist. He soon realized that was not the case, and as a result he spent the majority of the pilgrimage in his room in a state of despondency.

I attempted to explain to him that Medjugorje was not ecumenical per se; it was not Catholic or Baptist or Lutheran. It was, rather, a coming together of the children of God. Later, I learned that a month after returning home, the

Lutheran pastor finally grasped the real meaning of Medjugorje. Suddenly the sense of peace and happiness he had seen in so many of his fellow pilgrims began to register. He became a fervent witness to Medjugorje's good fruits.

I closed most of these talks in Northern Ireland by pointing out that in the face of ethnic and religious divisions, in the mire of distress experienced by those lost in the darkness of today's world of sin, the Virgin of Medjugorje was saying to all of us, "You are my sons, you are my daughters!" She came to this little village in obedience to God to lead us to her Son, Jesus Christ. And she was bringing the same message to Ireland.

The people I addressed in Northern Ireland were left with the thought that the message of Medjugorje is, above all things, a renewal of the gospel message. It is a call for reconciliation for people of all faiths, all ethnic backgrounds, and all levels of society.

For just as the body is one and has many members, and all the members of the body, though many, are one body, so it is with Christ. For by one Spirit we were all baptized into one body—Jews or Greeks, slaves or free—and all were made to drink of one Spirit.

—I CORINTHIANS 12:12-13.

18

Live My Messages

A crowd estimated at 100,000 filled the township of Medjugorje to celebrate the eighth year of daily apparitions. They listened with reverence, basking in the joy of being there on this special day in June 1989 as the Blessed Virgin gave this anniversary message: *Dear children, today I call you to live the messages which I have been giving you during the past eight years. This is a time of grace and I desire the grace of God for every single one of you. I am blessing you and I love you with a special love. Thank you for your response to my call.*

Millions more throughout the world anxiously awaited the message. They had become followers of Medjugorje through these monthly messages, which were leading them on the same path of conversion as those fortunate enough to go there. Eight years of good fruits had brought the apparitions to this point. Now, every book, video, and newsletter spawned by the phenomenon was eagerly received and passed on to family and friends.

Out of the spreading of the messages came a new way to "make pilgrimage" to Medjugorje. The month before the eight anniversary celebration in Medjugorje, the first national conference in the United States on Medjugorje was held at the University of Notre Dame, in Indiana. More than 5,000 followers of the apparitions came to enjoy three days of retreat into holiness—very much akin to what takes place during pilgrimage at Medjugorje. They attended Mass, prayed the rosary, and heard testimonies given by people who had found the path of spiritual conversion through the apparitions.

I was blessed to be a last-minute inclusion on the guest speaker list at the Notre Dame conference. With a time slot of only fifteen minutes, I told my story. This would be the first of many Medjugorje conferences that would become a mainstay of speaking invitations for me.

Within two years, similar conferences were springing up throughout the United States. Franciscan priests stationed at the parish in Medjugorje, and several of the visionaries themselves, were now coming to speak at these conferences, bringing their experiences to thousands who could not personally go to Medjugorje. Many skeptical and cautious priests and bishops who had journeyed there now urged the faithful to listen to and live the messages.

In August 1989 a huge celebration took place in Medjugorje. Young people gathered there from all over the world for the first organized youth festival, the Year of the Youth, celebrated in Medjugorje, as requested by the Blessed Mother. The festival coincided purposely with the Blessed Virgin's special feast day, the Feast of the Assumption.

Late that night on Podbrdo Hill, the Virgin came in apparition for the second time that day as several thousand young people crowded together among the rocks and shrubbery. They were anxious to hear the words of the Virgin Mary, who gave this message to two of her visionaries: *My dear children, tonight, I am very, very, very happy!*

The visionaries explained later that they had "never seen Our Lady so radiantly happy!" The reason for her joy was simply that her appearances were bearing fruit, and that people, especially young people, were responding. She asked that the Year of the Youth be extended into the coming years as an annual event, adding that she would like to also call it the Year of the Family. There, in that message given to thousands of youths gathered in Medjugorje, was the assurance that the Blessed Virgin would continue coming to Medjugorje at least through the next year.

This message came at an appropriate time, because just days before the first gathering of young people in Medjugorje, the local bishop had issued an order to the Franciscan priests at Medjugorje forbidding the visionaries from going to the choir loft of Saint James Church for the daily apparitions. There would be no more special apparition room within the church. No more priests were to be allowed to be present during the time of the apparition, no sick and handicapped pilgrims, and no media representatives. Panic set in among villagers and followers of Medjugorje. What would they do? Was this the end of the apparitions?

Such fears were soon put to rest as the apparitions continued. It seemed that if only by the sheer number of consecutive appearances, the Virgin's plans would be accomplished in spite of all obstacles. She continued to ask in her messages for the faithful to exert patience, understanding, and acceptance of such obstacles, even though we do not understand them. In other words, we must apply the messages to our daily lives. In time she usually shows us why certain things happen.

I am reminded of a beautiful story that occurred that

October while I was in Medjugorje. I stayed at Marija's home, and was pleased that a mutual friend, Paolo Lunetti (who would later become Marija's husband) from Italy, was also staying there. After greeting me, Marija asked me to accompany Paolo to pick up her sister Ruska and Ruska's baby and bring them to Medjugorje from Ljbuski, a small town about 12 miles from Medjugorje. Marija was not feeling well, and for that reason her daily apparition would take place in her home that evening. She wanted her sister there for the apparition.

I must admit that, somewhat selfishly, I was happy she wasn't feeling all that well: This meant that her daily encounter with the Blessed Virgin Mary would take place there in the living room of her home, and I would be lucky enough to be present. I could hardly wait.

We drove Ruska and her six-month-old baby to the house. Shortly after our arrival, one of Marija's nieces, five-year-old Ivana, entered the home, followed a little later by one of her nephews, six-year-old Philipe. Within minutes, there was the usual mass confusion created by little children at play. The apparition time was approaching, and I began to wonder how we were going to have such a holy miracle take place in such a distracting setting. Marija hardly noticed the noise as she began to make preparation.

Amidst the bustle and noise, Marija's mother and father came into the room. A thought struck me. I asked Paolo if Marija's parents had ever been with her in the apparition room, and he told me they had not. Now their faces were beaming, because they were going to be there with their daughter as the mother of Jesus came in apparition.

This was the setting: Marija, kneeling in front of a small statue in her tiny living room, began the rosary while the children continued running, laughing, and playing. Ruska's baby was crying loud and long, while Marija's mother and father were praying with added fervor. Paolo and I were attempting to do the same. The scene just described continued until just moments before the apparition.

All at once, Marija motioned for Ivana and Philipe to come and kneel beside her, one on each side. They suddenly became very quiet. The baby stopped crying almost as if on cue. There was instant peace and a sense of awe as Marija stopped her prayer in mid-sentence, and went into a state of ecstasy as the Blessed Virgin once again appeared to her.

I managed to glance at Marija's mother and father; the look on their faces was priceless. To see them so joyful to be present during this miracle was a joy in itself. In about two minutes, the apparition was over.

Immediately, the children returned to their games, and the baby was crying again. However, Marija was beaming. She told us that the Virgin had come with three cherub angels, a practice that usually occurs only when she appears to the visionaries on Podbrdo Hill. The Virgin looked at the little children in the room and said to Marija, *And you, also, have three angels with you!*

The Virgin then looked at each of us, Marija continued, and blessed us and then gave this message: *I wish for you to deeply live my messages I have given you.*

In that instant, all of the events of the past several months came together. The bishop had taken the apparitions out of the choir loft of the church and, indirectly, had placed them in the living rooms of the visionaries. Now their families could be present for the apparitions. The lesson the Blessed Virgin had been trying to teach us was being put into practice: to make this the year of the family, to pray together as families, and to attempt to live the messages in our families as well as in our personal lives.

This was where praying the rosary was to take primary importance; this was where we were to fast and do penance: in our families, with full family participation! In an instant, in Marija's living room, it became vividly clear what the Virgin was saying to us and showing us. She desired that we attempt first to live the messages with our families, and then carry it over into our communities, our work places, and our schools.

During Mass at Saint James Church on the last night of our pilgrimage, I noticed that there were more local people there than I had seen during the last several trips. That day was no special feast day or event. The people were simply there in the church, centering on the Holy Eucharist and on the beauty of the Mass. There was no apparition taking place in the choir loft, no flash bulbs popping, no one staring with hopes of seeing something supernatural. People were acting on what the Virgin Mary was asking, and they were putting the spiritual in first place in their lives.

In essence, we were being weaned away from the sensational and taught instead to rely on the spiritual.

That particular pilgrimage was one of the most memorable I had ever made to Medjugorje. But I will always remember the first pilgrimage with special fondness, especially the last day, when I had to leave and return to my home. I didn't want to leave; I wanted to stay in this heaven on earth. As I prayed behind the church on the last day of that first pilgrimage, just before I was to board the bus for the return trip to Dubrovnik, I felt myself being transformed into a spiritual child. Tears were streaming down my face from a strange mixture of sadness and joy.

Sitting on the side lawn for the final evening Mass of this latest trip, I watched people react in different ways. And I found myself in tears again. I realized anew how the Virgin was pleading with us, sometimes with bitter tears, to live her messages. Sometimes the tears were tears of blood because of the horrible sins of the world today. She wept because of the controversy over the apparitions and the lack of acceptance of them by many clergy, and by the world in general.

The repeated call in her messages was clear: We must make the messages come alive in our lives so that we can hear once again the Virgin's beautiful words to the young people on Podbrdo Hill: *My dear children, today I am very, very, very happy!*

To him the gatekeeper opens; the sheep hear his voice, and he calls his own sheep by name and leads them out. When he has brought out all his own, he goes before them, and the sheep follow him, for they know his voice. —JOHN 10:3–4.

19

Pilgrimage

As the final year of the 1980s began, I had just returned from a long speaking tour in the Philippines. Now I was doing the same in England and Scotland. In contrast to the overwhelming response by thousands in the Philippines, the response by the mostly modest crowds in the United Kingdom was much more subdued. Few seemed to know about Medjugorje's apparitions. Worse, people showed minimal interest. Making religious pilgrimage to the village where the Virgin Mary was reportedly appearing daily was hardly a consideration.

Except for a handful of people who had made the journey to Medjugorje, few knew about this supernatural event. They certainly didn't know me, an American Protestant who was speaking about an event usually reserved for Catholics. Thus, the audiences were composed mostly of die-hard Catholics, hungry for anything concerning the Virgin Mary. Scattered among them were a few curious Anglicans.

The speed with which word of Medjugorje was spreading

around the world was brought home to me 14 months later when I returned to the United Kingdom for a second tour. Once again, the tape of my 1987 talk in Saint James Church had preceded me. Much had changed. Medjugorje's apparitions were now better known throughout Britain. People of all faiths began to discover the good fruits of this unique miracle.

I began the fifteen-day excursion by plane, rail, and automobile. The tour would stretch from the northern tip of Scotland at Inverness, to North and South Wales; then it would continue throughout England, ending in London. I would be speaking in hallowed halls and churches dating as far back as the twelfth century, including a famous old church at Cambridge University.

The tour opened in a small town about an hour's drive from Manchester in England. It was bitterly cold, and I was suffering from jet lag, having just arrived from the United States that morning. The site at which I was to speak was a small hall in a Catholic school. When I found that it was packed beyond capacity, I forgot quickly about being tired or cold.

Two days later, an all-day session held in Manchester followed a format similar to what takes place each evening in Medjugorje at Saint James Church. Britons—Catholic and Anglican—came in droves, some from hundreds of miles away, and the church was again packed. The fervor I encountered throughout the day epitomized the attendees' high level of interest in Medjugorje.

In a whirlwind of train schedules, I managed to reach five more towns and cities before returning to Scotland for a weekend youth retreat at an out-of-the-way former hunting lodge in Dalmally. The lodge owners, Callum and Mary MacFarlane-Barrow, had made pilgrimage to Medjugorje. On returning to their home in Scotland, they were moved to convert their lucrative, well-known hunting lodge into a retreat center for personal spiritual pilgrimages. On that weekend, more than 70 young people were there from England, Scotland, and Wales.

Pilgrimages to Medjugorje from Britain were now taking place regularly. As in most places, the message of Medjugorje was desperately needed in the United Kingdom. The British suffered religious division as did so many other countries. The division was not outwardly noticeable or racked with violence as it was in Northern Ireland, but it was present. Fewer than twenty percent of the English were attending religious services of any kind; in Scotland and Wales, the figures were higher, but not by much.

There was strong resistance throughout Britain to efforts for unity among faiths. Worse yet, in one of her Medjugorje messages the Virgin Mary stated that England was the "center of the world" for abortion. That fact was justification for the need to reconcile people to God. And reconciliation did begin to take place. Pilgrimage to Medjugorje and other religious sites began to bring about conversion in the United Kingdom.

For the majority of Western nations, it was a strange phenomenon that religious pilgrimage should again become a popular fascination as it had been in earlier times. The great pilgrimage centers of Europe became thronged again, with much credit attributed to the apparitions at Medjugorje. The British, especially the English, were a bit dumbfounded by these happenings.

They shouldn't have been. The English are blessed with having one of the oldest Marian shrines, established to commemorate an eleventh-century apparition of the Virgin Mary. One of the earliest recorded accounts of a Marian appearance, that apparition took place in a large, beautiful manor in the small village of Walsingham, about an hour's drive from London.

Anglican nuns, who operate the Walsingham shrine along with Catholic nuns, made arrangements for me to speak there on my tour. The shrine itself is symbolic of the religious division in England; it is divided literally into two parts—one Catholic and one Anglican. I thought of the irony that this would be a site for spreading the Medjugorje message.

Walsingham owes its original fame to a woman named Richeldis de Faverches, the lady of the manor in 1061, who was in prayer one day when suddenly she had a vision of the Virgin Mary. She claimed to have been taken bodily to Nazareth in the Holy Land and shown the simple home where Mary and Joseph had raised the child Jesus. When the vision was repeated on two subsequent occasions, the noblewoman became convinced that she was being asked to build a replica of the home on her own land.

Lady Richeldis erected a replica of the holy house in Nazareth as it had been revealed to her in her dreams. Within a short time, the house became a center of medieval pilgrimage. It is said that the site on which the house was to be built was indicated by a spring of water, which appeared suddenly. Later, a statue of the Virgin Mary was made, based on Lady Richeldis's dreams; the image became known as "Our Lady of Walsingham."

Today, thousands of Christians, both Catholic and Protestant, flock to Walsingham. The apparitions of Medjugorje have brought about a renewed interest in this site where the Virgin once appeared. For me it was a special blessing to speak at this holy and ancient shrine.

As I flew home from this second tour of the United Kingdom, I thought of the statue at Walsingham. The infant Jesus is in the Virgin's left arm; her right arm holds a scepter, and her hand is pointing to her little Son, Jesus. I thought of how this pose signifies Mary's role as she leads us in pilgrimage to her Son.

His mother said to the servants, "Do whatever he tells you." —JOHN 2:5.

20

Fruits

In September 1989 Mirjana became the second visionary to marry. She and her new husband, Marko Soldo, arrived in Portland, Oregon, at the end of January 1990 to visit Father Milan Mikulic, who had performed the wedding ceremony in Medjugorje. This priest, who was originally from the Medjugorje region, had asked her to visit his parish so that other priests and his bishop, a skeptic concerning the apparitions, would know of this great gift of heaven.

While Mirjana was in Portland, the Blessed Virgin asked her by locution to prepare with prayer for a message the Virgin had for her. Mirjana entered the church, and as she started to pray, the Virgin again spoke to her by locution, asking her to leave the church and go into a small chapel in the rectory. She gently reminded Mirjana that the bishop of Mostar, whose diocese included her home parish of Medjugorje, did not want her to have her apparitions in a church since he did not personally believe the apparitions were real.

This was an important lesson. The Blessed Mother, the mother of Jesus, was in obedience to a bishop's order, and was telling her chosen visionary to do the same! Such obedience was a strong example to those who were testing the spirit to see whether the encounters with the Blessed Virgin Mary at Medjugorje were from God. Without obedience, there is no real spirituality. Without obedience, we cannot live the messages or guide our families to live them.

The message Mirjana received from the Virgin in apparition in the little chapel was a pointed reminder of the dangerous state of the world, as well as of the republics of the Federation of Yugoslavia. This is what the Virgin said: *I have been with you for nine years. For nine years, I wanted to tell you that God, your Father, is the only way, truth and life. I wish to show you the way to eternal life. I wish to be your tie, your connection to the profound faith. Listen to me!*

Take your rosary and get your children, your families with you. This is the way to come to salvation. Give your good example to your children; give a good example to those who do not believe. You will not have happiness on this earth, neither will you come to heaven if you are not with pure and humble hearts and do not fulfill the law of God. I am asking for your help to join me to pray for those who do not believe. You are helping me very little! You have little charity or love for your neighbor and God gave you the love and showed you how you should forgive and love others. For that reason, reconcile and purify your soul. Take your rosary and pray it. All your sufferings, take patiently. You should remember that Jesus was patiently suffering for you.

Let me be your mother and your tie to God, to the Eternal Life. Do not impose your faith to the unbelievers. Show it to them by your example and pray for them. My children, pray!

These words synthesized all the spiritual elements of the messages given in the course of the Virgin's appearances in Medjugorje. The division among ethnic groups in Yugoslavia now bordered on outright war. Clearly, a loving mother was admonishing her children.

Could the people not see where the present path was leading? Had she not warned them through her second appearance to Marija on that first day of conversation with the visionaries, imploring them to reconcile their historical differences? How was it possible for the priests who opposed the apparitions not to see the good fruits of these nine years of supernatural guidance?

Despite the intercession of the Virgin Mary through her messages, human hatred was seemingly immune even to the supernatural. Even in the church, some were blinded. It seemed as if Satan was on the verge of upsetting all of heaven's plans by destroying the framework of peace forged in nine years of work by the Queen of Peace.

But true to the mercy of God, the apparitions continued. The Virgin's pleadings only intensified, regardless of the refusal of so many people to listen. The divine obedience shown by the Blessed Virgin in asking Mirjana to receive her in apparition in a small chapel rather than in a church only added to the unofficial authenticity of the phenomena. The bishop was to be obeyed.

On March 25 the Virgin gave her monthly message to Marija, stressing that she was still there for her children's salvation: *I am with you, even if you are not conscious of it. I want to protect you from everything that Satan offers you, and through which, he wants to destroy you. As I bore Jesus in my womb, so also, dear children, do I want to bear you on to holiness. God wants to save you and send you messages through men, nature and so many things which can only help you to understand; but you must change the direction in your life. Therefore, little children, understand also the greatness of the gift which God is giving you through me, so that I may protect you with my Mantle and lead you to the joy of life.*

The year had begun in a war mode as the world hung on the edge of a potentially destructive clash in the Persian Gulf. Iraq was threatening to invade its neighbor Kuwait. The Blessed Virgin, appearing to address the situation directly, gave this warning in her first monthly message of the year (January 1989): *Dear children, today, like never before, I invite you to prayer. Your prayer should be a prayer for peace. Satan is strong and wishes not only to destroy human life, but also nature and the planet on which we live. Therefore, dear children, pray that you can protect yourselves, through prayer, with the blessing of God's peace. God sends me to you so that I can help you if you wish to accept the rosary. Even the rosary alone can work miracles in the world and in your lives. I bless you and I stay among you as long as it is God's will. Thank you for not betraying my presence here, and I thank you because your response is serving God and peace.*

In spite of the threat of retaliation from almost every oil-dependent nation in the world, Iraq indeed invaded tiny Kuwait. Iraq had drawn a line and dared the world to cross it. Could this be the start of another world war? The people of the world held their breath as an all-out invasion was launched to free oil-rich Kuwait. The call of free nations to defend against the invasion was successful. Kuwait was liberated, and within a week, peace was restored. Miraculously, a global disaster was averted.

In Yugoslavia, the threats of conquest turned into action; local clashes elevated to regional conflict. All-out war seemed a certainty. Here, the stakes were not for control of a precious world commodity such as oil. The commodity was human life and the right to freedom.

World leaders issued harsh condemnations and warnings to the Yugoslav leaders as sporadic clashes increased. However, there was no mass reaction or a coming together of nations as a unified army to protect the commodity of human life. In contrast to the case of Kuwait, the Western world, led by the United States, issued stern warnings that it would be "better" for the people economically if they stayed together in the Federation of Yugoslavia.

Were the people of this forced federation supposed to forget the oppression of years of brutal Communist rule or the inherent desire of all people to be free? Sadly, the motive for the West's reaction to the fomenting war in the Yugoslav federation was not the well-being of its people. There was no oil at stake. What was at stake was clearly and simply the loss of huge private investments in the economy of Yugoslavia— private investments by strong men, led by former government officials who had worked with the former Yugoslav regime.

In answer to the escalating threat of war within the Yugoslav federation, the Virgin's March 18, 1991 annual message to Mirjana once again pushed for the only true solution to human conflict: *Dear children, I am glad that you have gathered in such a large number. I would desire that you dedicate prayers for my children who do not know my love and the love of my Son. Help them to come to know it. Help me as Mother of all of you. My children, how many times I have already invited you here in Medjugorje to prayer and I will invite you again because I desire you to open your hearts to my Son, to allow Him to come in and fill you with peace and love. Allow Him, let Him enter! Help Him by your prayers in order that you might be able to spread peace and love to others, because that is now most necessary for you in this time of battle with Satan.*

The Virgin was identifying the real cause of the escalating conflict. She continued: *I have often spoken to you: pray, pray, because only by means of prayer will you drive off Satan and all the evil that goes along with him. I promise you, my children, that I will pray for you, but I seek from you more vigorous prayers and I seek you to spread peace and love which I am asking you in Medjugorje already nearly ten years. Help me, and I will pray to my Son for you.*

Among followers of the Medjugorje events, there was little doubt that the Blessed Virgin was continuing to address the war conditions. But again, the people did not listen. National pride rode roughshod over her words. On June 25, 1991—the tenth anniversary of the Medjugorje apparitions—Croatia announced its independence from the Federation of Yugoslavia, following the lead of Slovenia, which had successfully done so some months before.

Within hours, Croatia was in full war activity against insurgent Serbian forces, aided by the "official" Yugoslavian Army, comprised of men and women from all of the republics of the Federation. In a repeat of its attacks on Slovenia, the army attacked Croatia with intense ferocity. Slovenia had escaped with little bloodshed and damage because of its distant northern geographical location. Croatia would not be so fortunate.

Croatia's government leaders all but ignored the miracle occurring in neighboring Bosnia-Hercegovina, even though that miracle directly involved Croatian visionaries and villagers. Unprepared for war and armed only with national fervor and hunting rifles, the makeshift Croatian military plunged on in an attempt to break the chains forged by decades of Communist oppression, spurred on by the stunning example of other Eastern European countries. Within weeks, however, the dream of independence became a nightmare. Croatia soon after found itself in desperate need of essential supplies of food and medicine. Thousands were killed and thousands were more made homeless by the reality of active war.

On October 25 the Virgin gave the strongest of messages. She did not begin with her usual greeting of "Dear children." Nor, Marija stated, did she give her usual ending of "Thank you for having responded to my call." She only spoke three words, and she spoke them with great urgency: *PRAY! PRAY! PRAY!*

Too long have I had my dwelling place among those who hate peace. I am for peace, but when I speak, they are for war! —PSALM 120:6–7.

21

Answering the Call

Because of the threat of war engulfing Bosnia-Hercegovina, it was a harsh reality that pilgrimages to Medjugorje might soon be stopped by the very real danger of being caught in the conflict. Even in the fall months of 1991, few pilgrimages took place, and those that did were few in number. Another hard truth was that Medjugorje might never be the same. The call to conversion through the phenomenon of the Blessed Virgin's apparitions had, at least for the moment, been effectively muted.

The villagers of Medjugorje had to face the possibility that at some point in the future, pilgrims might no longer be able to come to their village. Somehow, that possibility seemed all right. The pilgrims would be missed, because the villagers and the pilgrims had become brothers and sisters under the motherhood of Mary. However, the Medjugorje experience that the Blessed Virgin was requesting for every pilgrim was to live her messages faithfully. It was not enough just to read them, or to say the rosary; it was not enough just to attend Mass as often as possible. She was constantly urging all that heard the messages to put them into action in daily living.

For the believer, there was another truth: If the messages were alive within them, then no one can bomb and destroy those messages. No one could take them away. Medjugorje thus became not just a village in Bosnia-Hercegovina where the Blessed Virgin Mary was appearing daily, but a way of fulfilling the call to holiness.

It could easily be said that this is why Jesus sent his mother to the tiny village: to create in each heart the symbol of Medjugorje—which is conversion to the heart to God. And that conversion comes through what happens to us spiritually when we answer God's call.

Such was the feeling of those intimately involved. The threat of war would not change that feeling. Those who had heard the messages in their hearts would continue to do their best to answer the Virgin's call.

I arrived in Medjugorje in August 1991, leading a small pilgrimage, including 12 teenage girls, most of whom were from my hometown of Myrtle Beach. Our arrival at a nearly deserted airport just outside of Dubrovnik was ominous. Airplanes had been moved far away and flights were at a minimum, in anticipation of actual war at any moment. Yugoslav gunboats lay off the coast in position to attack. When the attack would come was just a matter of timing.

I wondered again, as I had so many times leading up to the trip, why we were coming at this time. Common sense dictated that it was not safe, especially for teenagers, and most especially for teenage girls. But the pilgrims had insisted on coming—including the teenagers. And their parents were willing to allow me to bring them. All of them based their decision on their faithful attempt to answer the call of the Blessed Virgin. Most disconcerting was the parents' certainty that everything would be all right, because their daughters were going with me. The weight of that responsibility only added to my anxiety.

But in the setting of Medjugorje, it was hard to imagine that the threat of war could be as close as the beautiful snow-capped mountains surrounding the little valley. Flare-ups had escalated to full battles throughout Croatia, and rumors of troops congregating in these hills and mountains for an invasion of Bosnia, had me on edge. Worse was talk of clashes in and around Dubrovnik—and at the airport. I prayed that we would be able to leave at our scheduled time, with no problems.

Yet, as we arrived in the village there was nothing but joy and a sense of safety and inner peace. I was swamped with people asking questions and wanting to just talk. By the fourth evening of the pilgrimage, I desperately wanted to be alone. I had not even climbed Podbrdo Hill, the original site of the apparitions. My time had been consumed from morning until evening giving talks and listening to stories of conversion.

On this particular evening, I went to the back of the church, where a large outdoor altar had been constructed. I sat down in the last row of seats away from everyone, satisfied to be alone at last. I noticed two men and two women sitting in the front row near the outside altar. One of the men was bent over, and at first, I thought he was crying. As I silently joined in the praying of the rosary coming over the outside loudspeakers, I could feel that familiar inner nudge of Our Lady; she was speaking to my heart, saying, *You should go and pray over him.*

Many times when God asks something of us, we hesitate, letting our humanity keep us from saying yes. We hesitate to answer the call, even though it is hard to imagine we could actually say no when the message is so clear in the heart.

I sat there and compromised, thinking, "I'll just say a prayer for him from here. It's the same thing." The minute that thought formed in my mind, I knew it was wrong; but I rationalized that the man was not feeling well and would not want a stranger to interfere. I continued to pray alone, adding a prayer for him.

Suddenly, there was a tap on my shoulder. I glanced up: It was one of the women who were accompanying the sick man. She asked timidly, "I know people are always asking things of you, but I have a very special request. Could you please come and pray over that man up there in the front? Could you come say a prayer over him. . . ?" The young woman's voiced trailed off and she began to cry. "He's my brother and he is very sick. He has AIDS and he's dying. My mother and I brought him and his friend here, hoping for a healing."

I felt horrible, knowing I had hesitated to do what the Blessed Virgin was asking. I had failed in this particular instance to answer the call. Because of my hesitancy, it was too late to pray over him at that time. There was no real prayer in me. Offering a weak apology, I asked if she would bring him back to the same place the next day, telling her I would be glad to pray over him at that time.

The following day, they came. Both men had AIDS; the man who was so sick was Catholic, while his partner, who had been living with him for 17 years, was Protestant. The sick man was very repentant and open to what was happening in Medjugorje. He wanted a healing. The confused and frightened Protestant did not really understand what was going on. He knew nothing about Medjugorje or about apparitions, but he was hoping this was all real, because they had no hope left.

We prayed together, all of us, and then I put my arms around both of them and prayed to Jesus that they both might be healed spiritually and physically.

I wouldn't have done that for anything in the world five years before. I wouldn't have gone near anyone with AIDS, let alone pray for the person's healing. I would have judged him in my heart, and I would have condemned him. But the thought struck me: This was also war. It was the war of good against evil, the war that rages in all of us. And it was in these situations that Our Lady was urging us to answer her call. Her messages centered on the very words of Jesus when He said, "Whatever you do to the least of Mine, you do to Me." When we can see others as Jesus sees us and respond to them without judgment, then we can say we are answering the call.

The message given at Medjugorje was for us to become Jesus to one another. It meant accepting the sometimes uncomfortable tasks of administering to those most in need. For the people of Yugoslavia, it meant reconciling, even after years of bitter hatred, and after horrible atrocities had been committed in the name of nationalism. For everyone, it meant simply being Jesus to others and seeing Jesus in them.

This was a wonderful pilgrimage. Everyone, including the teenagers, felt the same love, peace, and happiness that others had felt before the threat of war.

The trip home wasn't easy. Arriving back in Dubrovnik, we found that our scheduled flight had been cancelled. Worse, there were no further flights for that day—or for the rest of the week. We were told that we would be put up in a hotel near the Adriatic coast. Now I was deeply concerned. That location would be right in the line of fire of the expected attack on Dubrovnik. As the adults huddled together trying to figure out just what to do, one of the young girls approached me with a suggestion: "Mr. Weible, we just came from Medjugorje and Our Lady tells us to pray and she'll take care of us. Why don't we do that?"

Out of the mouth of babes, I thought. Clearly, this young girl had heard the call. Immediately, we found a quiet corner and prayed the rosary. How Mary loves us, I thought! She continues to come to Medjugorje as the Queen of Peace and touch hearts, even into this stench of war. She comes to her children living there even though they are about to engage in horrible war.

Two hours later, after our travel agent had bargained with the Yugoslav airline officials, an aircraft was sent to transport us to Split, and then to Ljubljana, Slovenia, where finally we boarded a Lufthansa jet for Frankfurt, Germany. We stayed there overnight and found enough seats the following morning to return to the United States.

I didn't relax until all the teenagers were reunited with their families. For them, the intense situation in Dubrovnik and the extra day in Germany were exciting drama that only added to an already memory-packed trip. But the lessons these teenagers had learned at Medjugorje, and the memories they would retain of moving times of prayer on the steps of Saint James Church each evening, would far outlast the excitement of the last day for all of us. They had heard the call.

When I went to bed after returning to my home that night, I lay awake until very late, thanking Gospa again for the privilege of pilgrimage to Medjugorje—for the seventeenth time. Little did I realize that this pilgrimage would be my last for a long time to come.

There was again division among the Jews because of these words. Many of them said, "He has a demon, and he is mad; why listen to him?" Others said, "These are not the sayings of one who has a demon. Can a demon open the eyes of the blind?" —JOHN 10:19–21.

PART IV

Storm

For we are not contending against flesh and blood, but against the principalities, against the powers, against the world rulers of this present darkness, against the spiritual hosts of wickedness in the heavenly places. —EPHESIANS 6:12.

22
Crisis

Dear children, today I am inviting you to renewal of prayer in your families, so that way, every family will become a joy to my Son, Jesus. Therefore, dear children, pray and seek more time for Jesus and then you will be able to understand and accept everything, even the most difficult sicknesses and crosses. I am with you and I desire to take you into my heart and protect you, but you have not yet decided. Therefore, dear children, I am seeking for you to pray, so through prayer you would allow me to help you. Pray, dear little children, so that prayer becomes your daily bread.

The Blessed Virgin spoke these words of peace and assurance in her January 1992 monthly message. She was addressing all of her children throughout the world, but she was speaking most directly to the people of the former Yugoslav republics in the grip of an active war—a war that would soon spill over into Bosnia-Hercegovina.

With the people experiencing extreme anxiety and stress, the very act of the Blessed Virgin continuing to come in apparition was reassurance that in spite of human failure, she remained with them. Sporadic rays of hope would break through as negotiations took place between the warring factions. Truces were signed, intended to stop the fighting and destruction. Some of the negotiations and the resulting truces were conducted in Medjugorje, now recognized by all involved as a place of special peace. By January 1992 fifteen such truces had been broken.

Outwardly, life seemed normal enough under the circumstances. Pilgrimages still occurred, though reduced to a fraction of the size of groups that had come prior to the hostilities. But the people came, in spite of the conditions. They came for the same reasons as pilgrims before them, but with an added mission: to help the war victims in response to the Virgin's plea.

Locally, some good did evolve from an obviously bad situation: Many "outsiders" who had come only to exploit the phenomenon for profit, began to flee the area. The construction of restaurants, hotels, and souvenir shops was halted abruptly. The village underwent a much-needed purging of the crass commercialism that had threatened to overwhelm the holiness wrought by the apparitions. Medjugorje soon returned involuntarily to the quiet, uneventful life of pre-apparition days.

While the change was welcome, in reality it was the quiet before the storm.

In February, the Blessed Virgin gave this message: *Today, I invite you to draw still closer to God through prayer. Only that way will I be able to help you and to protect you from every attack of Satan. I am with you and I intercede for you with God that He protect you, but I need your prayers and* your "yes." You get lost easily in material and human things and forget that God is your greatest friend. Therefore, my dear little children, draw close to God so that He may protect you and guard you from every evil.

Through Mirjana's annual apparition on March 18, the Virgin gave this urgent warning: I need your prayers, now, more than ever before! I beseech you to take your rosary in your hands, now, more than ever before. Grasp it strongly, and pray with all your heart in these difficult times.

Less than a month later, on April 6, Bosnia-Hercegovina found itself in at state of war. The insurgent Bosnian Serbs, bolstered by the Federal Army of Yugoslavia, attacked with fury. Women and children began to flee their homes and their villages.

Churches, monasteries, convents, schools, hospitals, and historic sites became prime targets. These were the first to be destroyed mercilessly. Only 17 miles from Medjugorje, the city of Mostar came under constant shelling. The Cathedral sustained critical damage, while the bishop's residence and offices were bombed and burned. Bombs were falling on Citluk, only three miles from Medjugorje. For the first time in its history, Saint James Church was closed, boarded, and devoid of Holy Mass. Priests, nuns, villagers, and a straggling of pilgrims huddled in the basement of the rectory for services and for protection.

But the "Woman Full of Grace" was still there, still appearing to the visionaries. She continued to intercede for the people and to plead for prayers and fasting to end the fighting. In early May, bombs were dropped on Medjugorje—but they did little or no damage, many exploding high above the village, or falling into the surrounding fields without detonating. Two Russian-made MIG fighter jets were sent to destroy the village, especially Saint James Church. They came on a clear, cloudless morning, but as they approached their target, suddenly the valley was covered in dense clouds, and they could not see to drop their bombs. One plane was downed, while the other returned to its base. The surviving pilot, filled with superstitious fear and only a flicker of faith, defected from his military unit, knowing he had witnessed a miracle.

News of the war surrounding Medjugorje traveled quickly around the world. A huge information network had developed, without specific design, using telephone, fax, and Internet technologies. The network hummed with activity as news arrived. Prayer groups prayed with added intensity, attempting to comply with the Virgin's urgent plea. Tour companies wondered what would happen to planned pilgrimages. Former pilgrims worried about Bosnian families and individuals whom they had befriended during past pilgrimages.

On the home front, I continued with my speaking engagements. However, all my planned trips to Medjugorje had to be cancelled. Although I had gone there two or three times in each of several years, I could not justify going into an active war zone. Every article or television report on the crisis brought mixed feelings: I wanted to be there with the people who had become like family, especially the visionaries and priests. All I could really do was fast and pray for a swift end to the hostilities.

The questions asked at my speaking engagements now centered primarily on the war. What was happening in the village? Was it under attack? Were the visionaries safe? But the most frequently asked question was this: How could war occur in a place where heaven had sent the Blessed Virgin Mary to speak directly to mankind? That war could come to

Medjugorje was difficult for the believer to comprehend, much less for the skeptic.

Yet, the answer was clear: Humanity is free to choose. We choose to follow God, or we choose to follow Satan. We are soldiers for one side or the other in the classic battle between good and evil. The Blessed Virgin had given the warning in the first days, pointing out the necessity of reconciliation. The choice was there in every message, as she asked or invited or pleaded with us to live the messages; she never demanded or ordered us to do so.

In the beginning days of the apparitions I spoke frequently of Medjugorje, telling audiences how the village was spiritually pristine. That was the best way I could describe it: a place of holy exuberance, a place where thousands of hungry souls were coming from every continent to see and feel the peace. The village was the edge of heaven, and like so many that had made pilgrimage there, I wished I could stay.

In the following years, however, the pristine atmosphere began to show signs of polution: Pilgrimages began to include curiosity seekers and those who came strictly as tourists. Travel agencies, anxious to cash in on the growing popularity of the region, planned side trips for the purposes of purchasing goods or sightseeing in other parts of the country, taking pilgrims away from pilgrimage. The presence of the Virgin each evening became almost commonplace for many villagers who seemed to have forgotten the first days of this miracle of such great magnitude.

But all these happenings were to be expected. And in fact, if everything had been perfect from the early days onward, the Medjugorje events would have been suspect. Therefore, the human pollution soiling such an overwhelming supernatural event was no real surprise—but it was still disappointing. Many pilgrims who had experienced a life-changing conversion through Medjugorje were now busy following after every claimed visionary and locutionist. They seemed driven by an insatiable thirst to know every possible detail about any supernatural event. The monthly messages given to Marija were now awaited more out of curiosity about what new things might be said, rather than out of a desire to learn from them and make them part of daily life.

Sadly, I related to audiences in the years following the initial apparitions, Medjugorje had become a place of material opportunity for many. New entrepreneurs were coming to the village in droves. Their demeanor was that of rapacious wolves disguised as converted sheep, as they attempted to cash in quickly on the desires of those in search of miracles. Cafes and souvenir stands sprang up almost overnight, along with hotels and barracks. There was constant construction as villagers continued to build additional rooms onto their homes to house pilgrims. Many villagers who had responded so fervently in the beginning months of the apparitions were now busy making money as they had never made it before. They were too busy to attend evening Mass, or to pray a family rosary, or to fast on Wednesdays and Fridays as requested by the Virgin.

One could only wonder why God continued to pour out His Holy Spirit for such an unprecedented length of time, particularly in light of the fact that the majority of the world still did not know about Medjugorje's miracle. How could the apparitions possibly continue, especially since it was so evident that Satan was also there?

Each year brought greater gifts from heaven. Yet, with the addition of each new business, each new room, and each new souvenir shop, it was as if Satan were delivering blow after blow to the spiritual body of Medjugorje. And then, I pointed out to the audiences, came the greatest blow: war—

bloody, pain-filled, havoc-wreaking, killing war, the total unpeace of Satan.

I told of how political change in Yugoslavia, spurred by the collapse of Communism throughout Eastern Europe, had led to this final blow. At first there was rejoicing that democracy and freedom were at last at hand. But shocked disbelief followed as free elections and new governments were trampled by the remnants of Communism left in the Serb-dominated Yugoslav government. Federal troops invaded Slovenia, then Croatia, and finally Bosnia-Hercegovina. The forces of hell had now broken loose in an attempt to cap abruptly the fountain of grace flowing from Medjugorje.

After ten years of apparitions, pilgrimage to the village was effectively stopped; only the die-hards dared to venture into what was now a war-ravaged countryside. Bombs fell on and around Medjugorje but somehow, they did little or no damage to the church, to the hill where the Blessed Virgin had first appeared, or to Cross Mountain. Yet, homes and businesses on the road leading to Medjugorje were damaged or destroyed, as were other entire villages. But regardless of its seeming immunity from the devastation of war, for all intents and purposes, Medjugorje was shut down. It appeared that Satan had won.

The major questions being asked by those attending conferences at which I spoke were these: Would Medjugorje survive the war? They were referring not just to the physical Medjugorje, but to the spiritual Medjugorje. Would it continue to feed spiritually a world starved for authentic love and peace? I told them the answer depended entirely on whether we truly answered the call that had been sounded by the Blessed Virgin for nearly eleven years.

Bluntly, I repeated over and over, it was a time for a new commitment. Here, I related, is how the Virgin put it in her

March 25, 1992 monthly message to the followers of Medjugorje: *Dear children, today, as never before, I invite you to live my messages and to put them into practice in your life. I have come to you to help you, and therefore, I invite you to change your life because you have taken a path of misery, a path of ruin. When I told you "Convert, pray, fast, and be reconciled," you took these messages superficially. You started to live them and then you stopped because it was difficult for you.*

Know, dear children, when something is good, you have to persevere in the good and not think, "God does not see me, He is not listening, He is not helping." And so, you have gone away from God and from me because of your miserable interests. I wanted to create of you an oasis of peace, love, and goodness. God wanted you, with your love and His help, to do miracles and thus give an example.

Therefore, here is what I say to you: Satan is playing with you, and with your souls, and I cannot help you because you are far from my heart. Therefore, pray, live my messages and then you will see the miracles of God's love in your everyday life. Thank you for responding to my call.

Thus, it was clear that because of "our own miserable interests," Satan and the world were able to enter Medjugorje and to win a part of it. He was responsible for the war, using prideful, nationalistic hatreds as kindling. Those living there who had been blessed to be part of the gift of grace, failed to respond with fervor to her calls to pray and fast and accept penance. This failure allowed Satan to take The Miracle, and turn it into The Lie.

But as always, I related to the audiences, the Blessed Virgin had the answer. She gave it in her April 25 monthly message: *"Today also I invite you for prayer. Only by prayer and fasting can war be stopped. Therefore, my dear little children, pray and by your life give witness that you are mine and that you belong to me, because Satan wishes in these turbulent days to seduce as many souls as possible.*

Therefore, I invite you to decide for God and He will protect you and show you what you should do and which path to take. I invite all those who have said yes to me to renew their consecration to my Son, Jesus, and to His heart and to me so we can take you more intensely as instruments of peace in this unpeaceful world. Medjugorje is a sign to all of you and a call to pray and live the days of grace that God is giving you. Therefore, little children, accept the call to prayer with seriousness. I am with you and your suffering is also mine.

I reminded all who listened that there would be an end to the war. Medjugorje would once again thrive with new pilgrims, its resurrection serving as strong confirmation that this is indeed God pouring out His Holy Spirit on His people. Satan would be defeated, as he always is when he wages war with God.

The Virgin's plan was a plan of peace. Her plan would have prevented all of the horror if only her children had listened. As Vicka was quoted as saying, "The Blessed Mother said that she could stop this war easily if only we would pray and fast. . . ."

What causes wars, and what causes fighting among you? Is it not your passions that are at war in your members? You desire and do not have; so you kill. And you covet and cannot obtain; so you fight and wage war. You do not have, because you do not ask. You ask and do not receive, because you ask wrongly, to spend it on your passions. —JAMES 4:1–3.

23
Dark Fruits of the Battle

Sitting quietly in the cramped aisle seat of an airplane, I wondered what I was doing returning to Medjugorje. The war was raging—a dark, savage war filled with unspeakable atrocities. One could hardly imagine such horrors being done by humans to other humans. Suddenly, the thought struck me that it was January 25, 1993, the anniversary day of the apparitions, and the day the Blessed Virgin would give her monthly message to the world through Marija.

Just as suddenly, I knew why I was returning. The trip had a two-fold purpose: First, I needed to see firsthand the effects of the war. Father Svetozar Kraljevic, a Franciscan priest who often served as a spiritual guide to the pilgrims, and who was now a close friend, had urged me to come. Quietly and without drama, he pointed out that I did not know the Medjugorje of the war years. I had not seen first-hand how Satan's plan of attack was attempting to change the face of Medjugorje. How could I speak of this miracle, its messages, and the conversions that were occurring there even in the depths of evil's reign, if I did not come and see for myself?

Thus, after an absence of 18 months I arrived in the country that had become like a second home. Father Svetozar was at the airport in Split to greet me and to drive us to Medjugorje. We stopped briefly to deliver a cash donation to a priest who coordinated relief efforts in the region. The money was from people in my home parish in Myrtle Beach, South Carolina, many of whom had been to Medjugorje.

It felt especially good to give the money to this priest personally, knowing it would go directly to assist the most destitute. There were so many hungry and homeless families and individuals without hope, he told us, and they had precious little time to wait on slow-moving government agencies and charitable organizations.

As we drove, Father Svetozar spoke of similar relief efforts taking place throughout the region. Remarkably, millions of dollars in donations, food, and medicine were pouring in from many different countries. The sources were Medjugorje-based prayer groups and newly formed organizations operated by people who had come previously to Medjugorje on pilgrimage. Now they were returning to help the war victims, in direct response to the Blessed Virgin's frequent requests for penance. They were ordinary people—homemakers, businessmen, students—risking their lives to enter into active battle zones to help others.

As we drove the dangerous roads in what seemed the darkest of nights, the reality of war struck home. Frequent stops at heavily armed checkpoints, and many detours created by unsafe conditions due to active fighting, delayed our arrival in Medjugorje until the early morning hours.

In the village there was a feeling as different from that of the war-torn areas through which we had just traveled, as light is from darkness. There was an immediate feeling of peace, a sense of security and safety, a feeling of being "home" again. I was thankful to Father Svetozar for convincing me to come and see that in spite of the horror of war, the grace of Medjugorje was continuing.

There were noticeable differences from my previous visits. The morning after my arrival, I went to Saint James Church for the English-speaking Mass, only to find the church empty. On inquiring if there was to be an English Mass that morning, I was directed to the small room on the right side of the altar that had once served as the site of the apparitions. Inside was a small band of pilgrims, mostly Italians and a few Americans. Despite the cramped quarters and the diminished crowd, the holiness of Mass in Medjugorje was the same. That sparsely attended Mass was just as awe-inspiring as when thousands had filled and surrounded the church before the war.

After the Mass, I found a copy of the January 25, 1993 monthly message on the church bulletin board: *Dear children, today I call you to accept and live my messages with seriousness. These days are the days when you need to decide for God, for peace and for the good. May every hatred and jealousy disappear from your life and your thoughts, and may there only dwell love for God and for your neighbor. Thus only thus, shall you be able to discern the signs of this time. I am with you and I guide you into a new time, a time which God gives you as grace, so that you may get to know Him more. Thank you for having responded to my call.*

Reading the message several times, I knew the second reason for my return to Medjugorje. It was not just to see the results of the war, but to be a pilgrim once again. I wanted to climb Cross Mountain, and Podbrdo Hill where the Blessed Virgin Mary had first appeared. I wanted to sit in the church for long periods of time and pray. I wanted to just be in the presence of God.

But there was work to do. Father Svetozar was to drive me into the city of Mostar for an up-close look at the dark fruits of war. It had to be now, as he was leaving in two days to attend to efforts to raise more relief funds. Waves of anxiety and fear intermingled with a gauntlet of emotions as we made our way cautiously along the bomb-scarred road that led to the city.

The war scenes resembled those I had seen in pictures, only they were far worse: Mostar had sustained massive damage, as severe as that reported in Sarajevo. It seemed, Father Svetozar told me, that every time repairs were started, the shelling would be renewed. Serb forces, hunkered down in the surrounding mountains, lobbed shells daily into population centers, shopping areas, churches, and hospitals. The entire scene would be forever etched in my mind as I stared at a crater-sized hole in the side of a new hospital building. The former hospital administrator, a Serbian, was now in the hills assisting in the shelling of the hospital and its clinic.

I stopped taking notes and just looked at the destruction of what had once been a thriving city and a tourist attraction. Parks had now become cemeteries. Mounds of rubble rose where apartments used to stand. Hotels served as command posts and headquarters for the media.

There was no need to record every detail. These were, as in all wars, the terrible fruits that come without the true peace of God. The opening words of the January message came to mind: *Dear children, today I call you to accept and live my messages with seriousness. . . .* This was the result of not taking those words seriously, of not praying or fasting or attempting to reconcile. The hatred and jealousy that stemmed from misguided ethnic pride was shutting out the love of God.

Back in Medjugorje, I did manage finally to climb Podbrdo, scurrying up the small hill just a half-hour before leaving for Split and the return flight home. There was time for only a few, very intense minutes of prayer. Everything I had experienced in the past 17 trips to Medjugorje seemed to flash before me. I wept out of joy that Mary had allowed me to return—not just to witness the dark fruits of battle—but for these precious moments spent at the very spot where she had first appeared to the children. I thanked her for the reminder that only through prayer, fasting, and penance would the war come to an end.

A month later, having completed a speaking tour in Italy, I was with Marija and her fiancé Paolo Lunetti at his parents' home in Monza, Italy, when she received the February 25, 1993 monthly message. We began the rosary and prayed the first four decades. Marija then knelt in front of a small statue of the Blessed Virgin Mary. After several more minutes of prayer, the Virgin came in great peace and stayed for about four minutes, giving Marija the message. I could feel the peace and indescribable love as the Virgin blessed us before leaving in a cross of light.

Father Slavko Barbaric, Marija's spiritual director, telephoned from Medjugorje just past six o'clock to receive and record the message. It would then be scrutinized carefully for scriptural and doctrinal compliance before being translated into numerous languages for distribution worldwide. After so many years, this procedure had become the routine.

This was one of several times I witnessed Marija receiving the monthly message. Each time reaffirmed the incomprehensible grace being poured out to the world through the apparitions. Marija stated afterwards that Our Lady was very quiet and peaceful during the apparition.

Here is the message given that day: *Today I bless you with my motherly blessing and I invite you all to conversion. I desire each of you to decide for change in your life and that you work more in the church, not with words, not with thoughts, but with your example. Let your life be a joyful witness of Jesus. You cannot say you are converted because your life must become an every day conversion. To understand what you have to do, little children, pray and God will give you to know what you have to do concretely and where you need to change. I am with you and keep you always under my mantle.*

A month later (March), she gave this message: *Today, like never before, I call you to pray for peace: for peace in your hearts, peace in your families and peace in the whole world, because Satan wants war . . . wants lack of peace . . . wants to destroy all which is good. Therefore, dear children, PRAY! PRAY! PRAY!*

Remarkably, even with the war at its zenith, the good fruits of the miracle of Medjugorje continued to unfold. The Blessed Virgin was addressing directly both the war and the fruits of the message, as can be seen in the first three monthly messages of 1993. She implored the people to change their way of life, not just with words of prayer, but with actions. Putting prayer into action, she said, is the only way to true happiness and union with God. In the strongest of terms she warns of the dangers of allowing Satan to take away that peace and happiness. She also assured the people that she would not desert them. The apparitions would continue until

God's plan through Medjugorje was successfully completed.

The village itself remained a cool spot in the middle of an inferno. However, less than 12 miles away, a defensive front was established and the war raged. Men from the village would go for short periods of time to join in the defense of their country before returning to local jobs and family. Buses carrying them to the front lines would stop in front of Saint James Church, where the men would pray a decade of the rosary. Almost every soldier wore a rosary around his neck. In July, the first soldier from Medjugorje was killed in action.

The visionaries carried on with the task of spreading the messages. Marija had just returned from a speaking tour in Brazil. She was never comfortable speaking in front of crowds, not even in Medjugorje when pilgrims came to her home. Now, she had toured Brazil, speaking in front of thousands. In obedient humility, she had accepted this personal penance in direct answer to the Blessed Virgin's plea to witness to the messages.

At this time, the plans that were announced for Marija and Paolo Lunetti to marry in September, gave cause for concern among the Franciscans of Medjugorje. Would this marriage disrupt the flow of monthly messages, or the pattern of the apparitions, especially since Marija would be living in Monza, Italy? Marija attempted to assure them that she and her husband would be visiting the village frequently, and that nothing concerning her part in the daily appearances of the Virgin would change, as far as she knew. However, concern remained. The other visionaries who had married had settled in the village. Marija would be the first one to be living away from the direct spiritual guidance of the Franciscans.

At this point, Ivan was touring Australia, witnessing before thousands and doing an excellent job. The shy young man now spoke confidently about family values and prayer, stressing the need for young people to find the path of spiritual conversion.

Even Jakov, always reluctant to be on public display, was in Italy giving talks. In April, he too was to marry; his bride was a beautiful Italian girl whom he had met when she came to Medjugorje on pilgrimage. They would settle in the village and eventually begin taking pilgrims into their home.

Meanwhile, Vicka remained in Medjugorje doing what she had done so well for more than eleven years–serving as unofficial ambassador to the few remaining pilgrims coming to Medjugorje. How many times had I seen huge crowds in and around her modest home, gathering to hear her story and have her pray over the sick! On this recent trip, I passed by her home one day and observed her giving a talk to only two pilgrims. Her enthusiasm was the same as when the crowds were in the hundreds.

June 25, 1993 marked the twelfth anniversary of the apparitions, and astonishingly, nearly 30,000 pilgrims were present. The crowd included approximately four thousand people from the United States, and many thousands from Slovenia, Croatia, and Bosnia-Hercegovina. It was an incredible display of faith that so large a crowd would travel into an active war zone; theirs was a pure response of love and belief.

In response to the huge turnout, the Blessed Virgin gave this anniversary message: *Dear children, today also I rejoice at your presence here. I bless you with my motherly blessing and I intercede for each one of you before God. I call you anew to live my messages and to put them into life and practice. I am with you and bless all of you day by day. Dear children, these times are special and, therefore, I am with you to love and protect you, to protect your heart from Satan and to bring you all closer to the heart of my Son, Jesus. Thank you for having responded to my call.*

Even in the midst of the dark fruits of battle, the Virgin came to plead, to warn, and to reassure.

For you were called to freedom, brethren; only do not use your freedom as an opportunity for the flesh, but through love be servants of one another. For the whole law is fulfilled in one word, "You shall love your neighbor as yourself." But if you bite and devour one another take heed that you are not consumed by one another. —GALATIANS 5:13-15.

24
Martyr

Not all of the people traveling to Medjugorje went as pilgrims in the true sense of the word. Such was the case of Collette Webster. Collette did not join an organized pilgrimage; in fact, she did not even know about the apparitions of the Blessed Virgin Mary taking place in the little village, or of the global impact they had created.

This young woman did not go seeking answers to troubling spiritual questions or looking for direction in life. Instead, the 27-year-old American from Michigan traveled to Medjugorje in January 1993 on a personal mission to help the victims of the war in Bosnia-Hercegovina. She went there especially to help the children who were victims of the war.

Nine months later, this young woman, who had no special ties to the cause or its people, was killed by a sniper in the city of Mostar, moments after tending the critical wounds of a Croatian soldier. She saved his life and lost her own. She gave the greatest of gifts and fulfilled all that is asked by the Blessed Virgin Mary through her apparitions in Medjugorje.

In return, Collette gained one of heaven's greatest distinctions: She became a martyr.

Collette's mission began at home in the tiny town of Sunfield, Michigan, when she met and befriended a high school exchange student from Sarajevo. The young girl had been sent to the United States by her parents to escape the dangers of the war. As she spoke of the horrors taking place in Bosnia-Hercegovina, something clicked inside of Collette; she just knew she was supposed to go there and do what she could to help. Without a second thought, she made plans and preparations for the mission of her life.

Never too well organized in the past, Collette immersed herself uncharacteristically in a study of Bosnia-Hercegovina's geography and history, and the reasons for the current situation. She carefully read newspaper and magazine articles about the war, learning all she could. To prepare herself for her mission, she enrolled in an emergency medical training course at a nearby fire department.

Shortly thereafter, in September 1992, Collette told her father she intended to get rid of everything she owned and go to Bosnia to become a relief worker for the war victims. He was shocked—but not too shocked. John Webster's oldest daughter had always been different. As a child she was infamous for spur-of-the-moment actions, a trait that continued into her adult life as she jumped from job to job, drove too fast, and was involved in countless accidents. She ate poorly, chain-smoked, and suffered from asthma and insomnia. And she never seemed to stop moving.

Collette's personal relationships followed the same helter-skelter course. An ill-advised marriage to an older man already twice divorced ended predictably in failure—but on amiable terms. That was the only way Collette knew how to handle relationships. She had no enemies.

Having made the decision to go to Bosnia, Collette gave her car to her sister, sold most of her possessions, and signed over to her soon-to-be former husband full ownership of an old house they had purchased with the intent of renovating it themselves. This was another in an endless list of things planned but never accomplished. She also gave him outright ownership of a failing convenience store business they had started, the pressure of its operation having dealt a decisive blow to their marriage.

Such generosity under these conditions might be viewed as foolish or impetuous, but it simply highlighted another strong characteristic of Collette. Always sensitive and caring, she had a loving heart. Animals, people, charitable causes— anyone or anything she could love, she did.

In answer to her father's questions—why this cause? why this country?—Collette replied without hesitation: "Everybody sits and talks about problems, and nobody ever does anything. I just can't watch this happen. . . ." Before she left, she gave him a bookmark that read: "You never know until you try."

Resigned to her decision, Collette's family saw her off on her first-ever venture outside of the United States. She departed in January 1993 with a thousand dollars cash, a suit-case full of donated medicines, and a large duffel bag packed with food and clothes. Within weeks, part of her money had been stolen, and she had given refugees her wool socks and one of her two pairs of boots. She lived in a small room in Medjugorje, soon shared with four other relief workers.

Discounting the hardship she encountered, Collette dis-covered the pure joy of giving as never before. A stranger had told her on the plane to Zagreb to go to Medjugorje. There, he told her, she would find plenty of work to help the war victims. The stranger was right; within days of arriving in Medjugorje, Collette was fully involved in relief work.

She also discovered the miracle of the apparitions of the Virgin Mary, rekindling a weak flame of faith that had long lain dormant. Collette had been raised Catholic and knew a little about the faith, but had lost contact with God and the Church. Her parents divorced and remarried, going their separate ways. Somewhere along the way, her formal but infrequent church affiliation eventually settled at a Protestant church.

In Medjugorje, Collette was soon immersed in work at nearby refugee camps, orphanages, and hospitals. She became hardened to the constant thunder of guns and the gory realism of applying medical skills learned on the job, even assisting with an amputation. But these people, especially the children, captured her heart. It didn't matter whether they were Christian or Muslim. For her, there were no good people or bad people, no right or wrong political affiliation, in this tragedy; there were just victims. She didn't care which side they were on. Collette simply had to hug every child she saw. Without being conscious of doing so, she was living the Medjugorje message.

Noticeably changed, the young American volunteer returned home for a brief visit in June, staying just long enough to celebrate her twenty-seventh birthday and plead for finances to help the relief cause. She had been slightly wounded by a bullet that grazed her head as she assisted others to safety. A relieved family, thankful to have her home, saw other differences.

The unpredictable, impetuous Collette now radiated serenity, intermixed with fervent zeal for humanitarian service. She talked of going other places where she might be needed when this conflict ended. Her family had never seen her so focused—or so anxious to return to her mission. Around her neck, on a handmade necklace, she wore a plastic pacifier given to her by a little refugee girl, along with two bullet casings. These were perfect symbols of the struggle of which she was now a part.

News of Collette's involvement spread, and soon newspapers and other media were calling for interviews. When asked why she was involved in a conflict with which she had no personal affiliation, she replied, "I don't really know why. I'm Irish, I have no relationship to these people, but I've always been the type of person who stood up for the underdog."

Collette talked about the war, describing instances of shells exploding near and around her and other workers. She told quietly of refugees who had seen relatives raped, tortured, killed, and hanged, victims of atrocities beyond imagination or description. "You know it's happened," she said in one interview, "because you read about it, but when you meet someone who it's happened to, you still can't fully understand that person's plight unless you've been through it."

Filled with emotion, she spoke of little children coming into the refugee centers so shaken and suffering from shock that they attacked every stranger around them. "Kids seem to adapt easier than anybody," she said, "but they also seem to suffer the most long-term effects." Her joy, she added, was when these little ones could hug again.

Yet, she couldn't wait to return to her adopted people. Her next trip home would be for Christmas, she assured her family. But Collette would never return home again.

Frustrated in the ensuing months because of the lack of aid and finances, Collette took the final step in her mission. In early September, she joined the Croatian Army as a frontline medic so she could do more. On Sunday, September 26, approximately a year from the time she first told her father of her plans to go to Bosnia, she entered the last moments of her life's journey.

The day started on a happy note. Collette and several friends delivered a freshly baked apple pie to some soldiers on duty in Mostar. Later, she and the other volunteers entered a bombed-out building in an area notorious for fierce fighting. She found a young Croatian soldier near death from severe wounds. As Collette dressed the soldier's injuries, she was warned to stay low because snipers were active across the street from the building.

Finishing her task, she stood up without thinking, suddenly silhouetted in a nearby window. This was a foolish, impulsive action. Her army uniform became an inviting target, making her just another of the enemy to the unknown sniper. Suddenly, a loud gunshot boomed out, accompanied by a flash of light. The bullet ripped through her stomach. Collette slumped to the cluttered floor, her intestines exposed. As she looked at her wound, she calmly told her companions, "I'm not going to live." Moments later she added, "Tell my sister I love her."

Collette died several hours later on the operating table of the hospital where she had assisted other war victims so many times.

Her time in Medjugorje had not been spent climbing the hill where the apparitions first occurred, or scaling Cross Mountain. She did not spend every evening in Saint James Church at Mass, or join very often in the prayers of the rosary during her days in the village.

Collette was too busy living the message. She paid the ultimate price and received the ultimate reward of martyrdom.

Greater love has no man than this, that a man lay down his life for his friends. —JOHN 15:13.

25

What Then Is My Suffering?

War is the full presence of Satan and the total absence of God. The evil one always comes where the Virgin Mary is sent to bring God's peace. He comes to destroy that peace. He came to this land with the sole intent of destroying the fountain of grace pouring forth from Medjugorje.

As always, God creates light where there is only darkness. He brings forth good seed from utter desolation and hopelessness. This is the seed of the harvest.

What follows below is the bitter account of a devoted religious, whose tale illustrates graphically the horror of war that ravaged Bosnia-Hercegovina. It was not ethnic differences or opposing religions that caused this abyss of darkness; those were just the tools. Like all wars, this was a battle of greed and power and pride, another of the endless chapters of the same story.

In his fury, Satan singled out for attack, God's chosen ones, His brides who serve as consecrated nuns, whose sole purpose is to love Him in prayer and service. One particular voice rises above the others. She is a war victim of rape and its potential fruit of shame.

This is her response, given by way of a letter written to the superior of her convent. It is edited only for clarity and to protect the identity of the nun and her order. It states all that is necessary to describe the full inhumanity of this war. At the same time, it is an incomprehensible response that can come only through total conversion to God.

It is the perfect response to Medjugorje's message.

Dear Mother,

I am one of the novices who was raped by the militant Serbs. I am writing to you in regard to what happened to my sisters and me.

Permit me not to give you any details. It was an atrocious experience, incommunicable except to God, under whose Will I placed myself during my consecration to Him as I made my vows. My tragedy is not only the humiliation I was subjected to as a woman, or the irreparable offense against my choice of existence and to my vocation, but the difficulty of inscribing deep in my faith, an event which is certainly part of the mysterious Will of the One I still consider to be my Divine Spouse.

Only a few days before, I had read a dialogue of the Carmelites of Bernanos, and the thought had come to me to ask our Lord to let me die a martyr. He took me at my word.

I find myself today in a dark interior anguish. They have destroyed my life's plan, which I had considered permanent; now, they have traced another, which I have not yet succeeded in unraveling. In my teens, I had written in my private diary: "Nothing is mine; I belong to no one and no one belongs to me." Yet, one night, which I do not want to remember, someone took me and wrested me from myself and made me his.

When I came to, it was daylight. My first thought was of our Lord's agony in the Garden of Olives. A terrible struggle took place with me. On one hand, I asked myself, why did God allow me to be broken to pieces and destroyed precisely where I had placed my reason for living. And, to what new vocation was He leading me on this new path?

I got up, exhausted, while I helped one of my sisters, and then I got dressed. I heard the bell ring at the Monastery next to ours. I made the sign of the cross and mentally recited the liturgical hymn: "At this hour, on Golgotha, the True Pascal Lamb, Christ, pays the ransom for our sins to redeem us."

What then, Mother, is my suffering and the offense endured, in comparison to that of the One to whom I promised a thousand times to give my life? I said slowly, "Your Will be done, especially now that I have no other support but the certainty that You, Lord, are at my side."

I write to you, Mother, not to seek your consolation, but your help in giving thanks to God for letting me join millions of compatriots, offended in their honor, and to accept this maternity not wished for. My humiliation is added to that of the others, I can only offer it in expiation for the sins committed by the unknown rapists. And for peace between two opposing peoples then offering it to God's mercy.

Do not hold it against me if I ask you to share with me a "grace" which may seem absurd. These past months, I shed all my tears for my two brothers, assassinated by the very ones who terrorize and attack our towns. I did not think my suffering could be worse or that the pain could reach any greater dimension.

Every day, hundreds of scrawny-looking people, trembling with cold and bearing a look of despair, knock on the door of our convents. A few weeks ago, a young girl of 18 told me: "You do not know what dishonor is."

I thought hard about what she said and knew that it was a question of my people in pain, and I was almost ashamed of living close to all this suffering. Now, I am one of them. One of my people's many anonymous women whose body is torn to bits and whose soul is ransacked. The Lord has made me penetrate into the mystery of this shame, and also to the Religious that I am. He has accorded me the privilege of understanding the diabolical force of evil.

I know that from now on, the words of courage and consolation I will try to speak from my poor heart will be believed, because my story is their story, my resignation, strengthened by faith will be, if not an example, of some help to confront their moral and emotional reactions. God has chosen me—may He forgive the presumption—to guide these humiliated people toward a dawn of redemption and freedom. They will not doubt the sincerity of my intentions since like them, I too come from the frontier of abjectness.

I remember that during my studies in Rome, a professor of Slavic literature had read to me this verse by Alesej Mislovic: "You must not die, because you were chosen to be on the side of light." On the night I was raped by the Serbs, I repeated this verse which was like balm on my soul when despair threatened to destroy me. Now, it is all over and it seems as if it were a bad dream.

All is past, Mother, and now all begins. When you called me on the telephone with words of consolation, for which I will always be grateful, you asked me this question: "What will you do with the life placed by force in your womb?"

I felt your voice tremble while asking this question to which there was no immediate answer. Not because I had no thought of the choice I had to make, but because you did not wish to cloud my decision. I have made my decision now. If I become a mother, the child will be mine and no one else's. I could entrust him to others but he has the right to my motherly love, even though he was neither desired or wanted.

We cannot separate a plant from its roots. The grain, fallen into the soil, needs to grow where the mysterious Sower scattered it. I ask nothing of my Congregation, which has already given me everything. I thank my sisters for their fraternal support, especially for not asking embarrassing questions. I will leave with my child. I do not know where, but God, who suddenly shattered my greatest joy, will show me which path to take to accomplish His will.

I will be poor. I will don once more the old apron and clogs which women wear on working days, and I will go with my mother to collect the resin from the pine trees in our forests. I will do everything in my power to break the chain of hatred, which destroys our countries.

To the child I am expecting, I will teach only to love. My child, born from violence, will be a testimony that forgiveness is the unique greatness that glorifies a person.

Here, in the wake of the destruction of a way of life and a vocation of faith by the most hateful of crimes against a woman, we find the very essence of the messages given by the Blessed Virgin at Medjugorje.

To live her messages is to plant a seed that gives more than a thousandfold.

". . . My God, my God, why hast thou abandoned me?"
—MATTHEW 27:46.

26
Oasis of Peace

What can be said of this place that escaped the all-destroying wrath of war? Only that its survival, its preservation as a true oasis of peace, stood out starkly as miraculous in itself. After nearly three years of intense fighting, there had been no major damage to Medjugorje or direct confrontational attacks on the village. Now, in January 1994, the war continued to rage throughout the region at a furious pace, with action coming as close as three miles from the village. But the place of apparitions remained a sheltered place of peace and safety in the midst of a storm.

Daily life continued. Mirjana and Ivanka both were expecting babies in the spring. This would be Ivanka's third and Mirjana's second. Marija was expecting her first child in July. For the followers of the Medjugorje apparitions who were overly concerned with the predicted impending chastisements, the growing families of these three visionaries served as a positive sign. Two of the visionaries had received all ten secrets from the Blessed Virgin. They knew what was to come. Yet they chose to raise families. Mirjana would later be quoted as stating, "those with large families will be better off."

As if to confirm this sign of trust, the Blessed Virgin gave this monthly message in January 1994: *Dear children, you are all my little children. I love you. But, little children, you must not forget that without prayer you cannot be close to me. In this time, Satan wants to create disorder in your hearts and in your families. Little children, do not give in. You must not permit him to lead you and your life. I love you and intercede for you before God. Little children, pray!*

Once again the Virgin was reconfirming her call for all who would listen to continue life as normal, but with prayer as the center. That lesson applied even in the time of horrible war.

While spared physical damage, the village suffered casualties. At least one soldier from the community had been killed on the front lines. Wives and mothers prayed for the safe return of fathers, sons, brothers, and husbands as they served periods of time on the front lines. They prayed for an end to this horrible disruption of daily life.

As if in response, Gospa gave this message in February: *I thank you for your prayers. You all have helped me so that this war may finish as soon as possible. I am close to you and I pray for each one of you and I beg you, Pray, Pray, Pray! Only through prayer we can defeat evil and protect all that which Satan wants to destroy in your life. I am your Mother and I love you all the same, and I intercede for you before God.*

Even greater hardship became the norm of daily life. Electricity and water were available for only a few hours each day, yet the faithful continued to turn out in large numbers for the evening Mass at Saint James Church. They prayed constantly for peace and for the soldiers, on Podbrdo Hill and on Krizevac Mountain, trekking to both places in organized groups. They had not lost their spirit.

The Virgin responded with this message in May: *I invite all of you to have more trust in me and to live my messages more deeply. I am with you and intercede before God for you, but also I wait for your hearts to open up to my messages. Rejoice because God loves you and gives you the possibility to convert every day and to believe more in God, the Creator.*

The villagers were surprised to see such a large number of pilgrims from many different countries present in Medjugorje for the thirteenth anniversary of the apparitions. The Virgin gave this message through Marija as the faithful gathered in the village on June 25: *Dear children, today I rejoice in my heart at seeing you all present here. I bless you and I call you all to decide to live my messages which I give you here. I desire, little children, to guide you all to Jesus because He is your salvation. Therefore, little children, the more you pray, the more you will belong to me and to my Son, Jesus. I bless you all with my Motherly Blessing and I thank you for having responded to my call.*

This anniversary was different in one aspect. Intermingled with the visiting pilgrims were scores of refugees from war-torn areas. Most came because of relatives living in the area. New rooms built to house pilgrims now served as their living quarters. This was now their oasis of peace and safety, albeit a far cry from the security of homes and farms that had been held by families for decades. But it was better than the hastily erected refugee camps dotting the landscape, all of them critically short of essential food and medicine, and crowded beyond capacity with thousands of homeless victims.

The year ended with a noticeable decrease in the fighting. Shortages of food and medicine continued; soldiers and civilians from all ethnic groups involved were still dying in war-related activities. United Nations troops were now stationed throughout the region, but were seemingly ineffective in stopping ongoing small skirmishes.

Small but deadly little battles raged not just against resisting pockets of insurgent Serbian forces, but now also between Croatians and Muslims. Out of necessity, these two groups had been forced to ally against the Serbs for survival and self-defense. Now, with thousands of ethnically cleansed Muslims descending on and settling in Mostar and other areas that were predominantly Croatian enclaves, the two sometime allies began inflicting the same ethnic cleansing on each other. Mostar in particular became a ferocious battleground.

Throughout the conflict, pilgrims continued to journey to the village, arriving with desperately needed clothing, food, and medicine. Medjugorje had become a major port of entry for these items, exceeding the amount of direct assistance of large charitable organizations. Many of the pilgrims—especially young people, predominantly from the United States, Italy, and the United Kingdom—traveled courageously into active fighting areas to take the vital supplies to refugees. They were not afraid; the Blessed Virgin had assured them through her current messages that she would protect them in their mission to help the unfortunate victims. Not one pilgrim coming to Medjugorje during the active war years suffered injury or death as a direct result of combat.[11]

With a large group of pilgrims present in the village during the week of Christmas, the Blessed Virgin gave this

Christmas Day message: *Dear children, today I am joyful with you and I pray with you for peace: Peace in your hearts, peace in your families, peace in your desires, and peace in the whole world. May the King of Peace bless you today and give you peace. I bless you and I carry each one of you in my heart.*

This was a message only the faithful could fully comprehend.

You did not choose me, but I chose you and appointed you that you should go and bear fruit and that your fruit should abide; so that whatever you ask the Father in my name, he may give it to you. This I command you, to love one another. —JOHN 15:16–17.

PART V

Harvest

The disciples came to Him privately and said, "Tell us...what will be the sign of Your coming and of the close of the age?" And Jesus answered, "... Nation will rise against nation ... and there will be famines and earthquakes in various places; all this is but the beginning of the birthpangs. Then they will deliver you up to the tribulation. . . . And many will fall away, and betray one another, and hate one another.

And many false prophets will arise and lead many astray. And because wickedness is multiplied, most men's love will grow cold. . . . For then there will be great tribulation, such as has not been from the beginning of the world until now, no, and never will be. And if those days had not been shortened, no human being would be saved; but for the sake of the elect, those days will be shortened."

—MATTHEW 24: 3-12, 21-22.

27
Response

Thank you for having responded to my call.

These were the words the Blessed Virgin Mary used to close each monthly message. No greater example of such a response can be given than the humanitarian actions taken by former and contemporary Medjugorje pilgrims to assist the war victims.

Why would ordinary people interrupt the normal flow of daily life to go into an extremely dangerous war zone to take aid to people they did not know? Government agencies warned them of the dangers; friends and family members begged them not to go. But a voice rose above the warnings. It was the voice of the Blessed Virgin calling her children to help others in a time of urgent need.

The call was explicitly clear in the monthly messages given throughout the period of intense fighting. In February 1995, even as the activity of war was mercifully winding down, the Virgin renewed her plea: *Today I invite you to become missionaries of my messages which I am giving here through this place that is dear to me. God has allowed me to stay this long with you and therefore, little children, I invite you to live with love the messages I give, and to transmit them to the whole world so that a river of love flows to people who are full of hatred and without peace. I invite you, little children, to become peace where there is no peace and light where there is darkness, so that each heart accepts the light and the way of salvation.*

The brave, obedient souls entering into the inferno of conflict were attempting to live the messages. They were the signs of peace where there was no peace; they were the lights where there was no light. Without this direct aid by people charged spiritually through the apparitions of the Virgin Mary at Medjugorje, Bosnia would be a desolate land of the living dead. Hundreds of thousands of innocent victims would have died from neglect. Countless more would have been homeless.

The only proper response to the call was, and continues to be, an unconditional act of love. Indeed, love put into action is a direct answer to the Blessed Virgin's call to love as expressed in her April 1995 message: *I call you to love. Little children, without love you cannot live, neither with God nor with brother. Therefore, I call all of you to open your hearts to the love of God that is so great and open to each one of you. God, out of love for man, has sent me among you to show you the path of salvation, the path of love. If you do not first love God, then you will neither be able to love neighbor or the one you hate. Therefore, little children, pray and through prayer you will discover love.*

The response began with a "suitcase brigade." Pilgrims coming to Medjugorje were encouraged to bring something extra to assist the war victims. Medicine and clothing topped the list. Additional pieces of luggage began arriving with every pilgrimage, and the little pieces turned collectively into a sizeable quantity of vital relief supplies.

Later, many pilgrimages included visits to nearby refugee centers where the pilgrims could personally deliver special gifts of love. Entire refugee families were "adopted" by families of the pilgrims who came to the village. Regular financial support each month by these families helped bring stability to destitute refugees, allowing them time and resources to regain normalcy in daily life.

Inspired by this initial response, individuals stepped forth to establish more organized efforts. Soon groups throughout the United States and other countries were working full-time to raise funds and supplies, filling large containers and sending them to Bosnia and Croatia by air and sea.

Caritas of Birmingham, of Birmingham, Alabama, a lay-operated organization formed in 1986 to specifically spread the Medjugorje message, was soon delivering aid by containers two and three times a week. It was the efforts of this organization that spurred others to form small groups and join in the work. Caritas alone was responsible for multiple millions of dollars in aid donated by people throughout the country. They are still continuing the work.

In my home town of Myrtle Beach, South Carolina, Bob Derr, deputy chief fireman, and Doctor Bill Greene, a urologist, combined their talents and fervor with those of a few others to obtain and refurbish six used ambulances and ship them to areas of Bosnia-Hercegovina and Croatia where they were vitally needed. Their project began with a few words uttered during a visit to our area by Father Svetozar, who spoke about the war and the critical needs of the region. When asked what one could do to help, he mentioned the terrible shortage of ambulances.

Within a few months, Bob had searched around the country, and had located several dilapidated ambulances that were no longer in service. Both men traveled long distances to drive the ambulances to Myrtle Beach. They then secured the services of a local mechanic, with both of them pitching in personally where they could, to assist in preparing the vehicles for shipment overseas. Not satisfied with this project alone, Doctor Greene obtained medical supplies donated by drug companies, and the two men packed the supplies into each ambulance to its limits prior to placing it in a shipping container.

The response to the Blessed Virgin's call came from other countries as well. In the United Kingdom, Bernard Ellis, a Jewish convert to Christianity, organized a network that sent millions of pounds of relief supplies via truck convoys, even donating the trucks themselves so that the work could continue locally. Ellis's organization, the Medjugorje Network Appeal, met with such a widespread response that convoys were leaving England for Bosnia two and three times a month. Two such convoys, one of which was accompanied by Medjugorje visionary Ivan, were operated entirely by women. The other included the young American Collette Webster, who would later die a martyr's death at the hands of a sniper in Mostar.

Similar programs were underway in France, Italy, Germany, and Poland. The same was true in distant Australia, New Zealand, and other nations of the Far East. Even the little island nation of Bermuda, a few hundred miles off the coast of North Carolina, responded with many aid containers.

There are hundreds more of such stories. Two in particular typify the ecumenical call of the Medjugorje message, as well as its impact on the world. Both of them strongly exemplify the response to the Blessed Virgin's call through Medjugorje.

Jeff Reed, a free-lance pilot living in Dallas, Texas, was first touched by Medjugorje while listening to a mother of 12 children give witness on how the apparitions had brought unity and conversion to her family. An Episcopalian, with no special religious fervor, Jeff felt the flames of conversion setting his heart ablaze as he listened to the woman's story. He began studying books, videotapes, and anything else he could find, having to do with Medjugorje. As a Protestant, Jeff had never known about the intercessory role of the Virgin Mary, or anything about apparitions; now, he couldn't get enough.

After attending a Medjugorje conference in Wichita, Kansas, and hearing a talk by Father Svetozar, who by this time was a frequent speaker on the Medjugorje conference schedule, Jeff was moved to go to Medjugorje. Once there, he traveled on to Konjic, Father Svetozar's parish, to ask Father Svetozar what he could do personally to assist in the relief effort, especially in the Konjic region. He was disappointed when the good priest told him to pray, put the relief effort in God's hands, and not make a campaign out of his efforts.

But the desire to help would not go away. He did not know where to start or how to raise money for a needy Catholic Church in former Yugoslavia, especially since he was not Catholic. Jeff sought the advice of four good friends and associates. One of them advised him to contact me, knowing I was close to Father Svetozar and the situation in Bosnia.

I was speaking at a conference held in the well known Basilica of the Immaculate Conception, in Washington, D.C., when Jeff first approached me. He had journeyed to the conference in hopes of meeting with me, with no prior contact. Somehow, we were able to meet for five brief minutes. The young pilot poured out his story and asked me what he should do to get started. To his dismay, I told him almost the same thing Father Svetozar had said. He needed to pray, and if it was meant to be. . . .

Jeff was crushed—and now very confused. The desire to help the church and war victims in Konjic was still burning bright, but my words did not contain the answers he was seeking. Utterly discouraged, Jeff nevertheless went below the Basilica into one of the many chapels to pray, just as he had been told to do. Having never prayed so intensely in his life, he asked the Blessed Virgin over and over to allow him to assist actively in the relief effort. If that meant sweeping floors or digging ditches, that was all right with him, as long as she would allow him to work for her Son. Suddenly, he received a clear message from the Blessed Mother: *I already have.*

Seven days later, Jeff was startled to receive a check in the mail from one of the four people from whom he had sought advice. The check was for $50,000. In the envelope was a note, which read, "If Medjugorje can change you, it can change anybody." It went on to state that the money was to help him get started in his relief work.

As far as Jeff was concerned, this was both the start and the finish. Shortly after receiving the large donation, he flew to Bosnia and delivered most of the money to Father Svet in Konjic, doing so under a special fund account, set up through his Episcopal church, named Saint David's. Little did he know what else God had in mind for this special fund.

As the war escalated throughout Croatia and later Bosnia, Jeff took the remainder of the money in the Saint David's fund and began organizing relief work. The fund later became an independent, non-profit organization called

Saint David's Relief Foundation. As of this writing, an amount in excess of 8.5 million dollars in aid has been raised and sent to Bosnia and Croatia. Operating with a small staff, the foundation continues to deliver a container load of relief supplies approximately every two weeks.

Jeff Reed is definitely working for the Blessed Virgin's Son. He has since converted to Catholicism, and has made numerous trips to Bosnia to coordinate the work of Saint David's Relief Foundation. As long as people continue to assist him with funds, he will continue. When the funds stop, he will take it as a sign that God has other plans for him.

Jim Flickinger, an attorney living in Grand Rapids, Michigan, tells his own story:

> Prior to November 1990, I considered myself a pretty typical guy. I worked hard at my job as an attorney, went home for the evening, spent time with my family, and watched television until it was time to go to bed. Every day was pretty much the same.
>
> This way of life continued until I received a copy of a series of articles written by a Protestant about a place called Medjugorje, where apparitions of the Blessed Virgin Mary were reportedly taking place. My wife read them aloud to me one day during a long automobile trip. I immediately questioned if this was really happening. As an attorney, I was skeptical and reserved judgment. But the messages that Our Lady was giving gripped my heart. It was a spiritual wake-up call.
>
> Reading the articles led me to want to read other books and watch videos about the apparitions. Soon we

were also attending special Medjugorje-centered conferences. My focus in life changed. In November 1990, I found myself in Medjugorje. When I say "found myself," I am not referring simply to physically being there. Rather, I began to discover who I am called to be by allowing Jesus, through the intercession of the Blessed Virgin Mary, to give me a new heart in place of my stony heart. Prayer, reconciliation, fasting, the Eucharist, and the Scriptures became a daily part of my life.

Since the trip to Medjugorje, I describe my life as one of "planting seeds." There were many little projects, but the most important seed might be our personal involvement with the refugees of the war in Bosnia-Hercegovina. I was joined by two friends, Jon Maxey and Bob Hiner, and we ended up making ten trips there during the war to arrange medical aid for Bosnia and Croatia. Through our efforts, done without training and only a burning desire to help where we could, we were able to deliver to Bosnia over five million dollars in direct medical aid.

The program was so successful that news of it reached the White House. In December 1996 President Bill Clinton was in the process of making a decision about whether U.S. troops should be sent into Bosnia. A representative from the White House telephoned my office, inviting the three of us to attend a special meeting at the White House with President Clinton, in recognition of what we had accomplished with our personal mission.

Initially, we were reluctant to attend. Personally, I disagreed with many policies of the President and his administration. I did not want to be a pawn in any political game. But it dawned on me that the invitation was extended on December 8, the Feast of the Immaculate

Conception, and the day of the meeting was to be December 12, the Feast of Our Lady of Guadalupe. I knew immediately that we were being called to plant another seed.

On December 12 we were sitting in the Oval Office at the White House with President and Mrs. Clinton, and three other people working on similar missions in Bosnia. We had preceded the meeting early that morning by praying just outside of the White House. Many friends at home were doing the same for us.

The meeting could not have gone better. There were questions about our projects, questions about the attitudes of people in Bosnia, and discussions about U.S. troops in the country. But more than half of the time of the meeting centered on the need for the people of *our* country to pray for peace. Military solutions had failed. Negotiations had failed. It was prayer that was needed just as Our Lady continued to ask in her Medjugorje messages. That is exactly what we told the President.

I had expected reserved reactions from the President and his wife when prayer was advanced as a necessary step in the Bosnian peace process. The response could not have been warmer. There were sincere broad smiles and vigorous nods of approval to the call for prayer.

Also interesting was President Clinton's reaction to our gift to him of a rosary blessed in Medjugorje. I expected he would thank us and perhaps set it on his desk. That didn't happen. He held it in his hands from the time we gave it to him until the time we left the meeting.

We also gave a special gift to Mrs. Clinton, a copy of the book, *Medjugorje: The Message*. As she received the book, she recognized it immediately and asked very sincerely, "Do you think something is really happening there in Medjugorje?"

The response from all of us was, "Yes, absolutely!"

Later, we had an opportunity to talk further with the other people who had been invited to the meeting. Two of them were very involved with Medjugorje. They also felt compelled to come to the White House meeting to emphasize the need for our nation to pray for true peace.

Sometimes we plant seeds and never really know if they germinate and produce good fruit. I knew that many good seeds had been planted in the White House meeting, but I had no idea of the immediate results. However, a little less than two weeks later, I turned on the television while getting dressed for church. The "Hour of Power," a religious program featuring the well-known Protestant minister Robert Schuller, was in progress. It quickly caught my attention when Reverend Schuller stated he had recently met with President Clinton. As it turned out, his meeting was on the same day we had met with the President. On the television program that morning, Reverend Schuller said that the first words out of the President's mouth were, "Ask our world to pray for peace in Bosnia-Hercegovina!"

We continue to return to Bosnia, working and praying with the refugees and trying to alleviate some of their problems. In these two years we have worked closely with Croatian, Muslim, and Serbian leaders in Sarajevo, in designing and installing a special park known as "Peace Park." All three sides agreed upon a location and to help in the construction of the park. It contains all of the best and most modern playground equipment and is located in an area frequented by the children and parents of all three nationalities. In the center of the park is a four-sided pole stating on two sides in Serbo-Croatian and two sides in English, "May Peace Prevail on Earth."

Somehow, the seeds of Medjugorje multiply; we need only plant them in our hearts, and then nourish them through prayer, fasting, the Eucharist, reconciliation. and the Holy Scriptures.

May the response continue.

And he said, "The kingdom of God is as if a man should scatter seed upon the ground, and should sleep and rise night and day, and the seed should sprout and grow, he knows not how. The earth produces of itself, first the blade, then the ear, then the full grain in the ear. But when the grain is ripe, at once he puts in the sickle, because the harvest has come."
—MARK 4:26–29.

28
From Darkness to Light

The response has continued indeed. Charity was evident everywhere as physicians, dentists, nurses, and a wide variety of professionals came to the Medjugorje region to donate time and equipment, to help the homeless and sick. There was an intensity in the air to reach out to all victims, a calm but steady intensity to reestablish in the village and in the entire region, the true peace that had been so powerfully entrenched before the war.

A year before, the Blessed Virgin had expressed deep concern in a message of admonishment given to Mirjana during her annual apparition on March 18, 1995. The message was a strong call to action: *Dear children, as a mother for many years now, I am teaching you faith and love for God. Neither have you shown gratitude to the dear Father, nor have you given Him glory. You have become empty and your heart has become hard, and without love for the sufferings of your neighbors. I am teaching you love and I am show-*

ing you that the dear Father has loved you, but you have not loved Him. He sacrificed His Son for your salvation, my children. For as long as you do not love, you will not come to know the love of your Father. You will not come to know Him because God is Love. Love, and have no fear, my children, because in love there is no fear. If your hearts are open to the Father and if they are full of love towards Him, why then fear what is to come? Those who do not love are afraid because they expect punishment and because they know how empty and hard they are. I am leading you, children, towards love, towards the dear Father. I am leading you into Eternal Life. Eternal Life is my Son. Accept Him and you will have accepted Love.

The apparition lasted ten minutes. The Virgin's face was serious but radiating with love, the intensity of which was so great that tears of emotion flowed from Mirjana. The message was clear and direct: More had to be done to alleviate the suffering of the innocent victims of war.

A year later, the same intensity was again reflected strongly in the Virgin's annual message to Mirjana: *Dear children! On this message, which I give you today through my servant, I desire for you to reflect a long time. My children, great is the love of God! Do not close your eyes, do not close your ears while I repeat to you: Great is His love! Hear my call and my supplication, which I direct to you. Consecrate your heart and make in it the home of the Lord. May He dwell in it forever. My eyes and my heart will be here, even when I will no longer appear. Act in everything as I ask you and lead you to the Lord. Do not reject from yourself the name of God, that you may not be rejected. Accept my messages that you may be accepted. Decide, my children, it is the time of decision. Be just and innocent of heart, that I may lead you to your Father, for this, that I am here, is His great love.*

A walk through the village of Medjugorje and its surroundings revealed that the people were listening. They were hearing and heeding the Virgin's call.

One example that reveals the villager's good faith can be seen on the other side of the Medjugorje valley, where a small collection of multi-unit houses and a beautiful kindergarten building have been constructed. This complex is an orphanage run by Franciscan sisters under the direction of Father Slavko Barbaric. The rooms in the home are warm and modern, providing an atmosphere as close to that of a normal home as possible. The orphans are those of parents killed in the war.

The orphanage opened without a lot of fanfare: There was no international effort to raise funds for its construction. There was no special assistance from the government or from international charities. It was simply another project, badly needed, taken on by the Franciscans, the villagers, and the visiting pilgrims.

Now there is light in the lives and futures of these children. Before, there was only darkness.

Just beyond Podbrdo Hill, near the home of Marija and her husband Paolo, stands a sprawling complex of buildings surrounded by a high stone wall. Originally a drug rehabilitation center, today the complex serves far more purposes. It is a place for the "poor in spirit." It is for the alcoholic, the displaced, the destitute, those whose lives have been shattered by the ongoing war of evil against good. Today the former drug rehabilitation center is known as the "School of Life."

Sister Elvira, an Italian nun who had started 27 similar centers in eight countries, opened the School of Life in June 1991. The diminutive but dynamic religious was sure in the first years of her coming to Medjugorje that such a center was the right response to the people's needs. It now stands as ongoing proof that the phenomenon of Medjugorje is an authentic request from heaven for the conversion of sinners. Hundreds of drug users and others with deep needs have received help from the center since its opening.

The School of Life began with a dream in the mind of Sister Elvira. The next step was the acquisition of the rock-strewn property on which the center was to be constructed. The center's first "building" was a large tent placed on the property. There was no water or electricity. The charter residents began digging and building, using the stones in the ground for the building blocks of the walls and floors. Today, the present occupants continue the work.

The work is extremely hard. Each work day begins with prayer and Holy Mass, followed by a light breakfast. Then the residents begin a full day of physical labor, no matter the weather conditions. This is the only treatment plan for the addicts, and now for the others as well. There are no doctors, psychologists or nursing aides. There are no medications or withdrawal drugs for the addicts or alcoholics. There is no entertainment—no television or radio, no cigarettes or alcohol. There is nothing but prayer, love, and hard work.

The cure rate for the drug addicts is an astounding ninety percent. The spiritual conversion rate is even higher. Those accepted into the program are required to stay a minimum of three years, with a request that they remain an additional two years to serve others coming into the program. Yet they are free to leave at any time.

Those who stay must follow the regimen to the letter. The residents pay no fee; the work is supported by charitable donations. Today the residents make a variety of gift items that may be purchased by visitors, among whom are now usually all pilgrims coming to Medjugorje.

Within the walls one can find hundreds of success stories in treating the residents. And that success leads often to success in bringing about their conversion. One resident in particular serves as a singular example of light overcoming darkness.

Kenny Alston, an African-American, was living in that darkness that is the absence of God's presence. He had done so for most of his life. After starring in college basketball, he was a fourth-round draft choice in the National Basketball Association. But a knee injury during his first year ended his career as a professional athlete.

Kenny's response to the loss of a promising career was to turn to hard drugs. Having been raised in the cotton fields of Georgia, he did not know how to handle the success and glitter of college and then professional stardom. After his career ended, his downhill spiral accelerated. He was married and divorced twice; he fathered a daughter whom he later abandoned. He was in and out of drug rehabilitation programs. All his life, Kenny had lied and stolen without remorse. He continued to do so to feed his drug problem. Nothing in his life seemed to work. Life for the former star athlete was filled with abject darkness.

After a year in one of Sister Elvira's centers in Italy, Kenny was accepted into the Medjugorje community in June 1994. At first, adjusting to life in the center was strange. Kenny had always been the center of attention because of his athletic ability, but here he was an ordinary pilgrim. He found that the Croatian language, the hard work, and the lack of amenities were difficult to handle. Yet, something special drew him to the center. "I went into the chapel on my first day here," he related, "and I heard these guys singing. My background is Baptist and we always had a lot of music in church. The songs I heard them singing inspired me to stay. All my life, everything I started, I had failed. I made up my mind right there that I wanted to finish this particular walk in life."

Adding to the difficulty, Kenny was older than most of the men there by nearly twenty years. "The community wants a change in a person, a change of mind, body, and soul," Kenny said. "They propose a life in prayer. It was difficult to live this but after two years here, I now understand. To the community, prayer is power and might. It gives one force to go forward."

The community believes in providence and in being completely self-sufficient. It was hard for Kenny to learn to obey others, particularly the younger guys in the community. He had spent 25 years of his life always taking from others. Now, he had to learn to be obedient, to be humble, to listen, and to give service to others. Here, everyone was family.

After two and a half years in the Medjugorje center, Kenny went back to the United States, to St. Augustine, Florida, to work with the new Community of Hope—Sister Elvira's newest center—that had been established there. It was Kenny's desire to spend two years in service to the new community, in order to give back to the community what had been given to him. Besides helping the residents with their physical needs, he also gave talks to them, promoting the process that can bring the desperate out of darkness and into light.

Today, Kenny Alston is a Catholic. In recounting his story, he states: "There are three dates in my life that are very important to me: my birthday, and June 21, 1994, the day I entered the community in Medjugorje. The third date is October 16, 1996. That is the day I became a Catholic."

Kenny's story is a clear response to the Blessed Virgin's March 1996 monthly message: *Dear children, I invite you to decide again to love God above all else. In this time when, due to the spirit of consumerism, one forgets what it means to love and to cherish true values, I invite you again, little children, to put God in the first place in your life. Do not let Satan attract you through material things, but, little children, decide for God, who is freedom and love. Choose life and not death of the soul. Little children, in this time when you meditate upon the suffering and death of Jesus, I invite you to decide for life which blossomed through the resurrection, and that your life may be renewed today through conversion, that shall lead you to eternal life.*

As always, she ended with: *Thank you for your response to my call!*

Besides this you know what hour it is, how it is full time now for you to wake from sleep. For salvation is nearer to us now than when we first believed; the night is far gone, the day is at hand. Let us then cast off the works of darkness and put on the armor of light.
—ROMANS 13:11-12.

29
With Prayer

It should now be clear that there is only one sure way to obtain the peace the Blessed Virgin refers to so many times in her monthly messages: It is through prayer. In the more than 18 years of her apparitions in Medjugorje, prayer has been her constant request. With prayer, as the Virgin told us in the first days of the apparitions in 1981, . . . *you can stop wars and alter the laws of nature!*

Prayer comes in many forms—words, songs, and blessings. For more than 12 years, I have been giving a special blessing from the Blessed Virgin at the conclusion of my talks. It is a motherly blessing, not to be confused with a priestly blessing, which only a priest can give.

I feel that the Blessed Virgin asked me to give to others her special motherly blessing. Thus, when I speak to groups of people about Medjugorje, I give this blessing individually to every one present, so that they can use it and pass it on to others who are in need of spiritual assistance. I do this by asking the members of the audience to raise their hands if they wish to receive the blessing. This special blessing from Mary comes through her intercession and is a gift of grace from the Holy Spirit.

The special motherly blessing was first given November 29, 1988, in Birmingham, Alabama, to Marija. Marija had gone to Birmingham to donate her kidney to her brother Andrija, who was slowly dying from a kidney disease. This was an act of pure love by Marija, an act that would move her brother to a strong conversion to God. As God would have it, I was with Marija that day in the home of Terry Colafrancesco, the head of Caritas of Birmingham, who had helped arrange the transplant operation.

During that apparition to Marija, the Blessed Virgin gave her this message: *Dear Children: Bless even those who don't believe. You can give them this blessing from the heart to help them in their conversion. Bless everyone you meet. I gave you a special grace. I want you to give this grace to others.*

The Virgin followed this message with her monthly message given to Marija on Christmas day, again at Birmingham: *Dear children, I am calling you to peace. Live peace in your heart and in your surroundings, so that all may recognize the peace, which does not come from you, but from God. Little children, today is a great day. Rejoice with me! Celebrate the birth of Jesus with my peace, the peace with which I came as your Mother, Queen of Peace. Today I am giving you my special blessing. Carry it to every creature so that each one may have peace. Thank you for having responded to my call.*

Years later, I received a letter from a friend who told me a beautiful story about the blessing, a story that took place in California in October 1996. It concerns a little girl named Jasmine, and recounts the tale of a wonderful miracle obtained through Our Lady's special motherly blessing.

Alfred Lee, a faithful Catholic Christian with a strong devotion to the Blessed Virgin, is a handyman who does small repair jobs. Al felt he had a calling to bless small children, and he had been doing so for some time. Al once read a book on Medjugorje and learned of the Blessed Virgin's special motherly blessing. It struck him like "a bolt of lightning," as he told it, and he started giving the blessing to all he saw who were in need of prayer.

In October 1996 Al stated that he was going through a black time spiritually. As always, he prayed to the Blessed Mother and to Saint Therese, the Little Flower, asking that his prayers be heard. He went so far as to request a sign of roses from Saint Therese as a confirmation that his requests were being granted. He began to notice that every child he saw would give him a beautiful smile; for Al, these smiles became the roses of confirmation he had requested.

Two weeks later, Al was called to repair a water leak under the kitchen sink in an apartment complex owned by his daughter. The tenants were a young Mexican family, Jose, Elizabeth, and their two small daughters, Elvira, three and a half years old, and Jasmine, only 14 months old. Al had done small repairs for the family before and knew them casually. Elvira was timid and seemed to be afraid of him, while little Jasmine was usually sitting in a high chair or lying on the couch or the floor. She never played and always appeared listless.

After inspecting the sink, Al told Elizabeth that he needed parts for the repair and would be back shortly. Jasmine was sitting in her high chair, and Elvira was standing next to her mother as he prepared to leave. He then did something he had never done before: He asked the mother if he could bless her and her children with the motherly blessing. "Oh, please give it to us," Elizabeth answered. "I've been praying so hard for my little girl—she has a sickness. . . ."

Al gave the blessing, left to purchase the part he needed for the sink repair, and returned a short time later. When he knocked on the door, little Elvira let him in and smiled at him, surprising him by her smile, since she had always seemed to be afraid of him. Elizabeth, the mother, was sitting on the couch across from the door, holding Jasmine in her lap. Suddenly, the toddler jumped down from her mother's lap and ran to him, holding up her arms. Startled, Al picked her up and kissed her on the cheek, and she kissed him back. Elizabeth now looked startled and began to cry.

Thinking he had done something wrong, the repairman started to apologize. But Elizabeth interrupted him: "Those are the first steps that Jasmine has ever taken! She has never walked before, and the doctors said she would never walk!"

The mother then explained to Al, through tears of happiness, that Jasmine was totally paralyzed from the waist down, and had no feeling in her legs due to a form of diabetes. Now she was running all over the living room.

The following day Elizabeth took Jasmine to her doctor, who confirmed that the child was completely healed, but warned that the disease and its conditions could return. Today, Jasmine continues to walk as a normal child.

There is an addendum to the story. At a book autographing session in October 1998 at the Irvine Peace Conference, I was startled when a man approached me, handed me a book to autograph, and thanked me for telling his story of little Jasmine's healing through the Blessed Virgin's motherly blessing. Busy with the task at hand, I politely acknowledged his thanks and turned to the next person in line. Suddenly, I realized that this was the repairman involved in the miracle. I quickly called him back to confirm that he, indeed, was Alfred Lee, the man who had given the blessing to little Jasmine and her family. Yes, he told me, and Jasmine and her entire family were also at the conference!

The following day, we were able to take special time to introduce Alfred and little Jasmine, along with her family, to the conference audience. Here, I told the audience as I held Jasmine in my arms, was living proof of God's grace in action through Medjugorje. Jasmine represented everything we read about, listened to, and desired for ourselves and others through the special motherly blessing of Mary at Medjugorje.

The power of prayer had once more altered the laws of nature.

Here is another story, one of my favorites, of the power of prayer:

In 1996 during a speaking tour in England, I was privileged to spend time with a very special teenage girl, Geraldine Loftus, and her parents, whom I had met six years earlier. We had met under the most difficult of circumstances. Only ten years old at that time, Geraldine was dying of cancer.

Having been diagnosed as having only a few months to live, Geraldine was reduced to skeletal frailty, with an ashen pallor and a total loss of hair resulting from chemotherapy treatments. Through the intercession of the Virgin Mary by way of an inner urging, I made a brief, unplanned stop at Geraldine's home to pray over her. That stop was to become for me one of the greatest lessons on the undeniable power of prayer. The lesson touched thousands of readers when I later wrote about Geraldine in my books and columns.

Now, here I was having lunch and sharing company with Geraldine and her family. I was filled with awe and joy as I marveled that the little girl who had been deathly ill with cancer was now 16, and was celebrating life with all the enthusiasm of her teenage years.

But I learned that once again Geraldine was suffering from a bout with cancer. Once again, her skin was of an ashen pallor, and she had lost all her hair. At first glance one would never have known that she was so ill. She wore a beautiful brown wig that fooled me when I first saw her. Her eyes were still full of life, just as they had been when we first met. There was evident love between the child and her parents, a love full of hope and confidence. There wasn't a trace of bitterness or pity.

Some may ask how it was that this child who was prayed for and seemed to be healed, suddenly was struck again with disease. Some may question whether she actually was healed. But I do not ask that question, and neither do her parents. Geraldine lived a wonderful six years more than she would have, had there not been belief, confidence, and trust in the power of prayer.

I remember vividly the first time I was asked to pray over someone dying of cancer. The request came in the early days of my mission, at a time when I was traveling to Ireland with my family to join an Irish pilgrimage to Medjugorje. I was scheduled to return a month later for a speaking tour.

When a small party was thrown in our honor, I was touched at such kindness, especially since my family was with me. Several minutes after we settled in, our hostess pulled me aside and told me of her neighbor, a young mother of six little children. Stricken with cancer, she had only weeks to live. Peace eluded her as she worried about who would care for her children and her husband. Would I take a few minutes to visit her and pray over her? the hostess asked.

I wanted to refuse, having never directly confronted the ultimate suffering of death. It was one thing to talk about the power of prayer, but quite another to actively believe and exercise it. Feeling totally inadequate, I nonetheless agreed to pray over the young mother. But inwardly, I was reluctant; I felt as if I were being dragged to the bedside of the dying mother. I pleaded silently, "Jesus, give me something easier to begin with, not this!"

Once at the bedside of the woman, I became calm. I looked into her eyes and was warmed by the confidence of her faith as she told me she was ready to die, but was struggling over the penance her death would bring to her little ones and to her husband. She had read about Medjugorje through my articles, and felt that God had sent me to her. After venting her fears and carrying on a quiet conversation with me, for what seemed a lifetime to me—though it was only a matter of minutes, she let out a long sigh and said, "Now I feel at peace!"

I hadn't done anything special; I hadn't said any magical words. But I had prayed fervently for her, to have strength to believe and courage to trust in the power of prayer. Instantly, the lesson was implanted in my heart. It was as though I heard Jesus saying to me: "Have confidence in Me. Trust in Me. Let Me work through your belief!"

A month later when I returned to Ireland, I learned that the young woman had died a peaceful death. The woman's entire family had stepped forward to assist her children and her husband. The woman who had asked me to pray over the ailing woman thanked me for helping her friend. I learned then that I ought never to hesitate again when asked to pray over someone.

Later, I prayed over another little girl who was suffering from an incurable disease. Within weeks, she made remarkable progress and seemed to be in remission, even though she retained and periodically suffered from the symptoms of the disease. The mother, who was filled with joy in the beginning, wavered whenever her child suffered from the symptoms. She never believed fully that her little girl was healed, even though she, like Geraldine, is still living and is full of life today. One mother is at peace; the other is not.

Are we to believe that Lazarus and the others over whom Jesus prayed, people who were evidently dead or dying, were not healed because eventually, death would overtake them? Is a healing based on a time scale? Of course not.

The Blessed Virgin tells us repeatedly to pray. She tells us to have confidence in God, to approach Him with the heart of a child, to accept whatever penance we are given, to accept totally the will of God. That is conversion. She reminds us to accept the will of God but to ask in confidence for healing, both spiritual and physical.

Geraldine does this. She now asks me to pray for the young friends she has met in the hospital, friends who are dying of the same deadly disease she has. She does not worry about herself, even though she wants life and clings to hope constantly. She knows she received a special gift, as do her parents, who accept their painful burden with calmness and confidence.

Listen to the words from heaven given to us by the Virgin Mary in her anniversary message of June 1997: *Dear children, today I am with you in a special way and I bring you my motherly blessing. I pray for you and intercede for you before God so that you may comprehend that each of you is a carrier of peace. You cannot have peace if your heart is not at peace with God. That is why, little children, pray, pray, pray, because prayer is the foundation of your peace. Open your heart and give time to God so that He will be your friend. When true friendship with God is realized, no storm can destroy it.*

Is any one among you suffering? Let him pray. Is any cheerful? Let him sing praise. Is any among you sick? Let him call for the elders of the church, and let them pray over him, anointing him with oil in the name of the Lord; and the prayer of faith will save the sick man, and the Lord will raise him up; and if he has committed sins, he will be forgiven.

—JAMES 5:13–15.

30
The Good Fruits

Another major change brought the apparitions a step closer to their culmination. That change occurred in September 1998 as Jakov, while in the United States along with Mirjana for speaking engagements, received his final apparition with the Blessed Virgin; during it, he received the tenth secret.

The Blessed Virgin came to him on September 12 in Miami, Florida. With a gentle smile, she said to him: *Dear child, I am your mother and I love you unconditionally. From today, I will not be appearing to you every day, but only on Christmas, the birthday of my Son. Do not be sad, because as a mother, I will always be with you and like every true mother, I will never leave you. And you continue further to follow the way of my Son, the way of peace and love and try to persevere in the mission that I have confided to you. Be an example of that man who has known God and God's love. Let people always see in you an example of how*

God acts on people and how God acts through them. I bless you with my motherly blessing and I thank you for having responded to my call.

Jakov cried for a long time. He had cried most of the previous day when the Blessed Virgin had first told him that the next day would be his final daily apparition. The normally jocular Jakov was subdued as he traveled throughout South Florida giving witness talks. Several days later, he traveled to the poverty-stricken nation of Haiti, where more than 70,000 people came to hear the message of Medjugorje. A quieter, more mature Jakov was beginning a new phase of service as an example of how God acts on people and how God acts through them.

With Jakov's final apparition, three of the original six visionaries were still receiving daily apparitions, while the Virgin continued to appear at least once annually to the other three. All but Vicka were now married, with Ivan marrying an American, Laureen Murphy, in October 1994. At the time of this writing, Ivan and Laureen now have two children. The theme of family remains strong as the new century approaches, and the grace of the daily apparitions continues.

On a mild early November afternoon in 1998, more than 700 pilgrims gathered in the huge, newly constructed hall some 200 yards behind Saint James Church. They were there for a talk I was giving primarily for English-speaking pilgrims. But word of the talk had spread, and many groups of non-English speakers were also present. The presence of so many pilgrims was visible proof that after more than 17 years of daily apparitions by the Blessed Virgin, good fruits continue to flow from Medjugorje.

On this, my twenty-eighth trip to Medjugorje, I had brought a pilgrimage of 220 people from across the United States. These pilgrims were the premise for the that afternoon's talk. As I began, a feeling of humility and awe filled my heart. Each talk always seemed as if it were the first, and in nearly 14 years of traveling the world to speak about the message of Medjugorje, I have never found the subject routine or dull.

In our group there was a family with an astounding 18 members present. I asked them to stand. The widowed mother had brought her children and their spouses and their children to Medjugorje as a family unit, spending what she called her "inheritance" to do so. She was convinced there was nothing better she could give them for their future. They clearly served as a powerful symbol of the theme of family that runs through the Blessed Virgin's messages.

A young Lutheran pastor and his wife were also part of our group. I also asked them to stand. They represented the ecumenical outreach of the Blessed Mother, who constantly emphasizes her untiring desire to bring all of her children to her Son.

I then asked how many pilgrims were in Medjugorje for the first time. To everyone's amazement, all but a few hands were thrust in the air. A low murmur ran through the crowd. "Do you realize," I asked them, pausing for a moment, "that the Blessed Virgin Mary has waited 17 years, four months and a few days for you to come to Medjugorje? Are you aware that the miracles, signs, and wonderment of the beginning days of the apparitions are just as abundant for you today as they have been for pilgrims since the beginning of the apparitions?"

The low murmur exploded into applause. The point was clear to this modern-day gathering of pilgrims: Medjugorje today is the same as Medjugorje in the early eighties. Conversion through prayer, fasting, and penance still occurs today as it did then.

With a merciful end of active war, a tentative peace prevailed. But signs of the "Storm" were still very evident. Several days later, our pilgrimage traveled by bus to Mostar to celebrate Mass in the new chapel at the Franciscan monastery. The trip allowed our group an up-close look at the fruits of war. We passed the cathedral with its roof still caved in from the shelling that pounded the city during the height of war in 1992. The bishop's home, which had suffered similar damage, had at least been restored and was occupied once again.

Our buses rolled past cemeteries that had been expanded beyond their original boundaries with hundreds of new tombstones. Many beautiful parks had been turned into cemeteries to accommodate the overload of casualties. Thousands of bullet marks riddled the walls of buildings that were still standing, while other buildings lay in ruin, serving as constant reminders that aid is still desperately needed. And it will be needed for years to come.

A drizzle of rain fell, making the mood of our trip more somber. The buses parked a good distance from the chapel in a makeshift lot near the new church building that was still under construction. We trekked in silence to the monastery. I was reminded of an earlier visit here with Father Svetozar during the war; at that time we had to run from doorway to doorway to avoid the lethal danger of snipers hidden in the surrounding bombed-out buildings.

By the time I reached the chapel, it was filled. Feeling a bit annoyed, I wondered aloud why we were assembling in this smaller chapel when there was a much larger sanctuary, located in the basement of the main church that was presently being used by the parishioners. One of our guides, Slavenka, a striking Croatian woman with blazing red hair, assured me with a smile, "Don't worry, it will hold us all. It is no different than being in Saint James Church for the evening Mass."

She was right. While there was hardly room to move, we all managed to find a niche. Eventually, my annoyance was replaced with peace. It was as if we could sense the full force of peace in this special place that had risen anew out of the darkness of the war. Because of its location, the chapel provided us with one of the holiest and most peaceful times of our pilgrimage. Here, surrounded by the remnants of the unpeace that had prevailed for so long, we had a holy encounter with the Prince of Peace.

After the Mass I spoke briefly, reminding the pilgrims that they were seeing firsthand the diseased fruits of the absence of love. This was visible evidence of the dark fruit of Satan, who is always lurking where Mary is sent, attempting to snatch away the grace. I reminded the pilgrims that the battle was not just the one played out in the killing fields of active combat. The battle was within each of us. It is the constant battle of good against evil. That is why Medjugorje continues today, I told them. This pilgrimage was a reminder, as were all of the others, that the battle rages on until every possible soul has the opportunity to say yes or no to God's gifts of grace.

Back in Medjugorje, I pointed out to the pilgrims how different the village looked from the village I had encountered on my first pilgrimage in May 1986. Aesthetic and practical improvements had been made to the church grounds, including the construction of the new hall and other new buildings for meetings and special services. But for the most part, the villagers were the same, and the pilgrims coming from countries throughout the world were the same. The evening program of prayer of the rosary followed by holy Mass still overflowed in attendance.

On the other hand, commercialism could now be seen everywhere; but that was to be expected. Humanity and its original stain will always be part of any supernatural spiritual event, as a reminder of the ongoing attempts by the forces of evil to conquer the good. Again, without that evidence of evil attempting to overthrow the good, one should be suspect of the authenticity of a purported supernatural event. The choice of good over evil is there for each to make, and the opportunity to make the choice is the same for every person.

During Mirjana's annual apparition in March 1997 the Virgin had reminded the people that we have a choice about which path we will take: *Dear children! As a mother I ask that you do not go on the path that you have been on, that is the path without love towards neighbor and towards my Son. On this path, you will find only hardness and emptiness of heart, and not peace, which you all long for. Truthful peace will have only that one, who in his neighbor sees and loves my Son. In the heart of the one where only my Son reigns, that one knows what peace and security is.*

She followed this message with another reminder, in her monthly message on the sixteenth anniversary of the apparitions, June 25, 1997: *Today, I am with you in a special way and I bring you my motherly blessing of peace. I pray for you and I intercede for you before God, so that you may comprehend that each of you is a carrier of peace. You cannot have peace if your heart is not at peace with God. That is why, little children, pray, pray, pray, because prayer is the foundation of your peace. Open your heart and give time to God so that He will be your friend. When true friendship with God is realized, no storm can destroy it.*

The Storm would always be part of Medjugorje's story. While active war had ceased and the battle for souls continued, the war of opposition to accepting the apparitions raged on.

In view of the continued opposition to the apparitions by many clergy, one must ask, are the opponents of the apparitions blind? Can they not hear or understand? Are six unsophisticated teenagers–now young adults, most married and parents—capable of maintaining a pretense of seeing a heavenly visitor for more than 18 years? Could a fabricated story give rise to millions of conversions to Jesus Christ across the entire world?

No apparition has ever had as large an impact on the world as Medjugorje. How could an act of the devil—as some opponents label the Medjugorje apparitions—lead to renewal of whole dioceses, the creation of thousands of prayer groups, the reconciliation of thousands of families, and the acceptance by so many of priestly and religious vocations?

The answer to these questions lies in the book of truth, Holy Scripture: ". . . because seeing they do not see, and hearing they do not hear, nor do they understand. With them indeed is fulfilled the prophecy of Isaiah which says: 'You shall indeed hear but never understand, and you shall indeed see but never perceive. For this people's heart has grown dull. . . .'"

And for those who do believe because of the good fruits, Holy Scripture says this: ". . . But blessed are your eyes, for they see, and your ears, for they hear. Truly, I say to you, many prophets and righteous men longed to see what you see, and did not see it, and to hear what you hear, and did not hear it" (Matthew 13:14–16).

What is the Church's stand on Medjugorje today? In August 1996 Dr. Joaquin Navarro-Valls, spokesman for the Holy See, issued a public statement in answer to charges that the faithful were being disobedient in going to Medjugorje: "You cannot say people cannot go until it has been proven false. This has not been said, so anyone can go if they want."

The apparitions remain under investigation by the bishops of Bosnia-Hercegovina, although their activity is basically dormant. A ruling on the authenticity of the Medjugorje events will not be issued until the apparitions have apparently ended, and the investigation is completed. However, again due to its fruits, Medjugorje is officially accepted as a shrine, a special place of prayer and worship.

Even Pope John Paul II has spoken unofficially in glowing terms of the good fruits of Medjugorje. The retired Bishop Sylvester Treinen of the United States told a Medjugorje conference crowd numbering in excess of 7,000 that the Holy Father gave this response when Bishop Treinen told him he had just come from Medjugorje: "Yes, it is good for pilgrims to go to Medjugorje and do penance. It is good!"

The Storm of evil, the Storm of unrest, subsides when we listen with open hearts to the Blessed Virgin's words, such as these given in her August 25, 1998 message: *Today, I invite you to come still closer to me through prayer. Little children, I am your mother, I love you and I desire that each of you be saved and thus be with me in Heaven. That is why little children, pray, pray, pray until your life becomes prayer.*

As she always does, the Blessed Virgin reaffirmed the entirety of the apparitions from their beginning right up to the present time, in her October 25, 1998 monthly message: *Dear children, today, I call you to come close to my Immaculate heart. I call you to renew in your families the fervor of the first days when I called you to fasting, prayer and conversion. Little children, you accepted my messages with open hearts, although you did not know what prayer was. Today, I call you to open yourselves completely to me so that I may transform you and lead you to the heart of my Son, Jesus, so that He can fill you with His love. Only in this way, little children, will you find true peace, the peace that only God gives you.*

The good fruits of the harvest continue.

So in the present case I tell you, keep away from these men and let them alone; for if this plan or this undertaking is of men, it will fail; but if it is of God, you will not be able to overthrow them. You might even be found opposing God! —ACTS 5:38–39.

31
The Final Harvest

Relatively little has been said to this point about the ten secrets given to the visionaries. The reason for that omission is simple: The Blessed Mother tells us to focus on the love, peace, and grace of the apparitions. She tells us that we are not to be concerned with the secrets beyond knowing about them. In an early message in answer to questions about the secrets, she replied, . . . *Place them in your mind and in your heart, and then pray for the conversion of the world.*

Her point is, if we live the messages, we have no reason to fear the future. Our focus in the time of final harvest should be on personal conversion to the ways of God. The purpose of the Virgin's lengthy visit is to grant all people the opportunity to find true peace and happiness. What if we knew the contents of all of the secrets? What would we do? Would we not pray and fast in hopes that all of our family and friends would respond through conversion?

We are given signs and wonders in Medjugorje to assist us in understanding and accepting that this entire event is of

God. The Blessed Virgin gave us so many signs in the early days, signs that continue to this day. The miracle of the sun still occurs in Medjugorje, and by God's grace, many people who have been touched by Medjugorje are able to see that miracle at times in their own communities when they return home.

The pilgrims who take the messages seriously, move beyond the signs. They are the ones who thank God and attempt to put the messages to work in their daily lives. We see, we acknowledge, and then we move forward spiritually. These are the souls who will be among the final harvest.

Of course, supernatural happenings are not confined to Medjugorje: Wondrous signs are being given in other places throughout the world. Recently, I learned about one such sign while in El Paso, Texas, for a speaking engagement. On the second day, with a little time off in the morning, several people from the group that sponsored my tour planned a trip for us into Juarez, Mexico, right across the border.

As we crossed the border, there were few changes in the landscape. Then, little by little, we could see the worst of the abject poverty of Mexico: the poor, shabby buildings and homes, the roads in desperate need of repair. We went into such a neighborhood with the purpose of visiting the home of a couple living in this poverty, but who had been blessed with a miracle of hope.

The couple had been an example of the lower levels of family life today. Though unmarried, they were living together in poverty and depression. The man, an alcoholic, would go into fits of exasperated rage brought on by the cross of being poor. It was rage that caused him frequently to beat the woman severely. The woman had been brought up as a believer but had fallen into this situation as she had become lukewarm in her faith.

In a desperate move to escape the horror of her daily life, the woman had purchased a large picture of the Sacred Heart of Jesus at a local flea market. The picture was tattered and stained. But she bought it, spurred by faint memories of her faith practiced as a child. Maybe, she thought, if she took it home and prayed to Jesus, her man would change.

The woman placed the picture on a small table in her bedroom and began to pray. Suddenly, she noticed blood running down the picture, flowing slowly from the Sacred Heart of Jesus vividly depicted in the picture. It was actual blood, and it was flowing profusely. Shocked, the woman called the man into the bedroom to see this miracle. In seconds, both fell to their knees, rubbing their eyes, overwhelmed with what they were seeing. Amid weeping and wonderment, they began to pray in earnest.

A short time later, with the miraculous bleeding still occurring, the man stopped drinking and stopped beating the woman. They began attending church, went to confession, and shortly thereafter, they were married in the church.

Word of the miracle spread among the poor of the region. People came from everywhere to the run-down little neighborhood to see the wondrous sign of the bleeding heart of Jesus Christ. Priests came, the local bishop came, and scientists came. No one could explain why the picture bled. The blood was analyzed and discovered to be human blood. The heart in the picture would bleed most profusely on Thursdays and on holy feast days. Thousands came and continue to come to this day as the bleeding continues.

The purpose of our visit to the site of this miraculous sign was simply to see it. After being introduced to the woman who had purchased the picture and erected the little shrine, we knelt in front of it and began to pray the rosary. I sensed in my heart that this was a true sign. As we prayed, I felt the Blessed Virgin asking me to leave a medal from Medjugorje—a medal she had blessed during an apparition—at the site of this bleeding picture.

Concluding our prayers, I gave the woman a medal, telling her I wanted to leave another one near the picture. She was happy with this and told me through the translator that she and her husband had a small altar inside the house, and that it would be better to put the other medal there. We went inside where the woman had a small altar with a little piece of red velvet covering it and a crucifix lying on top. I laid the medal near the crucifix and said a quick prayer.

As we prepared to leave, one of the women from our group, not satisfied with where I had placed the medal, picked it up to move it closer to the crucifix. Suddenly, she let out a scream, telling us to come quickly and look. The medal from Medjugorje that I had placed just moments ago near the crucifix, was now bleeding!

Why would God give such a sign as this bleeding picture and medal? Possibly because after 18 years of miracles experienced through Medjugorje, and many more like this picture and medal, there are so many people who do still do not know that God exists, and that He loves us so much that He is willing to give such signs and wonders. There are millions of people throughout the world who do not know the peace, grace, and love that flow from the miracle of Medjugorje.

The messages from the Virgin of Medjugorje are not about punishment; they are about love and mercy. She does not come in apparition for one individual or one denomination. She comes for all of the separated brethren who call themselves Christian, Jew, or Muslim; she comes for all of the followers of God. She comes to bring us together as one family under the one God.

The secrets are not just about chastisements. We already have chastisements. We have abortion, drugs, and division. We have the division of the children of God. We are divided for the same reason great nations become fragmented: We have abandoned God and His laws of morality, replacing them with self-serving civil laws. We heap indignities upon ourselves as we scratch, claw, and connive to achieve the best and the most for ourselves. We want the richest of material goods, and the greatest power and authority.

In truth we no longer are able to say, "In God we trust." Now we say, "In Civil Law we trust." It is Civil Law, raised to secular holiness, that allows the "freedom" to deny God and His laws. It is Civil Law that legitimizes the heinous killing of innocent children in the womb, that creates endless loopholes for business to cheat and for individuals to bear false witness. It is Civil Law that encourages us to covet what others have in the name of success. It is Civil Law that breaks every commandment of God!

We are divided because we have abandoned the real laws. A little less than 70 years ago, mainstream Protestant churches accepted contraception as a legitimate practice, seeing it as using the intelligence granted by God to "limit" the size of families based on unwanted pregnancies and economics. In 1973, that "acceptance" was increased disastrously beyond measure when the right to an abortion became the civil law of the land.

Thus, contraception entered into a new, far more lethal stage. Today, 25 years later, more than 375 million abortions have taken place under the protection of law. That is a conservative figure. Only now is the awesome reality beginning to register. In the United States alone we have killed the equivalent of the entire population, plus 100 million!

We still do not seem to understand how division within God's family happened. We do not understand the schism that, nearly a thousand years ago, first split the Church into East and West, into Roman Catholic and Orthodox. We do not understand why the sixteenth-century attempt to reform a corrupt church hierarchy led to the departure of millions of the faithful from their Catholic roots.

It was not irreparable differences in theology or geographical separation of too great a distance that caused these divisions, and it was not one man or one cause. The division then and now is the work of Satan, plain and simple. He uses the weaknesses of man to divide and conquer; he uses pride, greed, and lust. His ongoing war to divide the creatures created in the image of God rages on in a desperate attempt to keep the love of God from being known.

The Blessed Virgin has given us the formula for being among the final harvest of souls through her messages at Medjugorje. She will not come to us indefinitely. We are living the sorrowful mysteries of the rosary. We are in agony, and we are suffering the scourging at the pillar. We are wearing the crown of thorns; we are staggering under the weight of the cross. We are approaching the crucifixion. We see the agony in our churches, in our daily life, in our families, and in our nation. We are not blind.

This is the time when we must choose between God and Satan. That is why God grants such overwhelming grace as allowing the human mother of Jesus to come to us for so long a time. This is the time just before the beginning of the things that are to come. We are asked through the Virgin's messages to place our hands on the cross with Jesus.

Conversion is surrender to the finality of crucifixion. When the last soul of the final harvest has had the opportunity to surrender to Christ and His cross, when cleansing has come, Jesus will not have to be depicted on the cross anymore. The true love of God will reign.

The time is now. At some point there will be just one visionary at Medjugorje still actively receiving apparitions from the Blessed Virgin. Then there will be none. When the last apparition takes place, there will be a brief period of time before the secrets begin to occur. For those who believe, it will be a time of joy—not apprehension or fear. It will be a fulfillment of what the Blessed Virgin said in the early days of Medjugorje: *When I have appeared for the final time to the last visionary of Medjugorje, I will no longer come in apparition to earth again, because it will no longer be necessary.*

For those who choose not to believe the grace of the apparitions, it will be too late.

When will the Blessed Virgin make her final appearance at Medjugorje? After more than 18 years of daily apparitions, is the time near? The answers lie only with God, but this much is known: The Blessed Virgin promised Lucia, the last living visionary of Fatima, that she would live to see the fulfillment of the secrets of Fatima; Lucia is in her late eighties. She has reportedly stated that Medjugorje's apparitions are a fulfillment of the secrets of Fatima.

Finally, as if the longevity and frequency of the Medjugorje messages were not enough, the Virgin has given the most revealing sign of the urgency of the times through an important message to Father Stefano Gobbi, founder of the Marian Movement of Priests. This powerful message was given to him at yet another famous apparition site, Lourdes, France, in September 1988.

Here are important highlights of that message that coincides precisely with the Virgin's long-running message of conversion at Medjugorje. That message to Father Gobbi authenticates the modern period of apparitions by the Virgin Mary as beginning with La Salette : . . .*On this day, I ask you to consecrate to me the whole of the time which still separates you from the end of this century of yours. It is a period of ten years. They are ten very important years. They are ten decisive years. I ask you to spend them with me, because you are entering into the final period of the Second Advent, which is leading you to the triumph of my Immaculate Heart in the glorious coming of my Son, Jesus.*

The Blessed Virgin Mary is speaking of a period of time that began 12 years ago! Thus, we are already in the final period of the Second Advent. She continued: *In this period of ten years the fullness of time which I have pointed out to you, beginning with La Salette right up to my most recent and current apparitions, will be completed. . . . In this period of ten years, the purification, which you have been living through for years, will come to its peak, and therefore sufferings will become all the greater for everyone. . . . In this period of ten years, the time of the great tribulation, which was foretold to you by divine Scripture, before the second coming of Jesus, will be completed. . . . In this period of ten years, the mystery of iniquity will be manifested, prepared for by the ever-increasing spread of apostasy. . . .*

The permanent sign will come, and the world will know the full truth of God's miracles, not only at Medjugorje but those He has performed throughout the ages. Many will say for the first time: "My God, You are real!" The signs will come, not just at Medjugorje, but at all the past apparition sites. After the signs have come and the secrets have been fulfilled, the world will be fresh, clean, and pure again.

And we shall then live as mankind lived in ancient times. That is what the Blessed Virgin said in the early days of Medjugorje. And we shall be the fruit of the final harvest.

Then I looked, and lo, a white cloud, and seated on the cloud one like a son of man, with a golden crown on his head, and a sharp sickle in his hand. And another angel came out of the temple, calling with a loud voice to him who sat upon the cloud, "Put in your sickle, and reap, for the hour to reap has come, for the harvest of the earth is fully ripe." So he who sat upon the cloud swung his sickle on the earth, and the earth was reaped.

—REVELATION 14:14–16.

The Final Mercy

After eighteen years of wondrous apparitions, great signs, and revealing messages being given at Medjugorje—signs and wonders that are continuing to the present—the final harvest nears its conclusion. And as the Blessed Virgin tells us, once the harvest has been gathered, humanity will finally live and worship God as in ancient days.

According to the Blessed Virgin, the last phase of the harvest is the fulfillment of the ten secrets, which fulfillment will not take place until she has made her last appearance at Medjugorje. Once the ten secrets begin to be revealed, a major piece in this mosaic of grace will be put into place, one that will reflect the entirety of the Medjugorje phenomenon and its revelation of God's unconditional love.

I believe this piece to be one of the first three secrets, which, as disclosed by the Blessed Virgin, are warnings to the world to prove that the apparitions of Medjugorje are truly from God. According to Mirjana, who was shown the first warning by vision (chapter 14), there will be a major upheaval in a region of the world. And, as described in earlier chapters, the third warning is the permanent sign that will be left at the spot where the Virgin first appeared. Thus, this last grace could conceivably be the second warning—or the second secret.

The entire phenomenon of Medjugorje is a gift of mercy. However, this last major piece in the mosaic of grace is a final Divine Mercy, given through the Holy Spirit, one that will allow every living soul an opportunity to receive the grace of peace and happiness through belief in and acceptance of the ways of God.

The grace of this Divine Mercy will be given in a unique way. Throughout the ages of recorded apparitions, locutions, and other supernatural spiritual phenomena, there has been a consistent thread of prophecy that describes an interior "illumination" of the soul, an illumination that will be experienced by every living human being at a designated time. Sometimes it is referred to as an illumination of the conscience. The illumination will occur at a time known only to God, and will suddenly permit every human being to see his or her soul exactly as God sees it.

Every sin committed will be visible to each individual soul, no matter how small or how great; every good deed done will be visible, no matter how small or how great. The world will stand still for a moment of time as this incomprehensible grace is given to all of humanity.

What will happen following the final Mercy is then up to each individual. Those who believe in God will experience great good from it, while those without belief will suffer with the pain of truth. Some will die of the shock of seeing themselves as God sees them. The final Mercy will reveal to all faiths that God truly exists. After the illumination it will be impossible to deny God's existence. Yet, each individual will still have the free will to accept or reject God. Sadly, there will be those who will reject Him.

Many examples from past and present claimed prophecies of the illumination could be listed here, but we need look no further for corroboration than the locutions given to Father Stefano Gobbi, described in previous chapters, which strongly mirror the messages of the Blessed Virgin at Medjugorje. Appropriately, on Pentecost Sunday, June 4, 1995, the Virgin gave this powerful message confirming the illumination: *Tongues of fire will come down upon you all, my poor children, so ensnared and seduced by Satan and by all the evil spirits who, during these years, have attained their greatest triumph, and thus, you will be illuminated by this divine light, and you will see your own selves in the mirror of the truth and the holiness of God. It will be like a judgment in miniature, which will open the door of your heart to receive the great gift of Divine Mercy.*

A year later, in May 1996 Father Gobbi was given yet another message concerning this final Mercy, one similar in tone: *Miraculous and spiritual tongues of fire will purify the heart and souls of all, who will see themselves in the light of God and will be pierced by the keen sword of his Divine Truth. . . .*

Therefore, even at the eleventh hour, every person will be given the opportunity to respond to the Virgin Mary's call from Medjugorje. It should now be clear that the Medjugorje messages are not about punishment, but about love: holy, divine love. They are simply an affirmation of Holy Scripture. It should also be clear that the final harvest is not one of doom, but an outpouring of God's unconditional love, as seen in this Divine Mercy.

God has sent the Virgin during these years for all people, all who call themselves Christian, Jew, Muslim, Hindu—

even those who call themselves atheists or non-believers. As always, she attempts to lead us in a gentle, motherly way, as reflected in this message given on September 25, 1998: *Dear children, I call you to become my witnesses by living the faith of your fathers. Little children, you seek signs and messages and do not see that, with every morning sunrise, God calls you to convert and to return to the way of truth and salvation. You speak much, little children, but you work little on your conversion. That is why, convert and start to live my messages, not with your words but with your life. In this way, little children, you will have the strength to decide for the true conversion of the heart. Thank you for your response to my call.*

In this message, as in the hundreds contained in this book, the emphasis rests on putting the messages faithfully into practice in daily life. The formula is always prayer, fasting, penance, and reconciliation. And the good fruits of living the messages are true peace and happiness. What more do we need?

May we be part of the final harvest of souls, and may it be a harvest of great abundance.

Then I saw a new heaven and a new earth; for the first heaven and the first earth had passed away, and the sea was no more. And I saw the holy city, new Jerusalem, coming down out of heaven from God, prepared as a bride adorned for her husband; and I heard a loud voice from the throne saying, "Behold, the dwelling of God is with men. He will dwell with them, and they shall be his people, and God himself will be with them; he will wipe away every tear from their eyes, and death shall be no more, neither shall there be mourning nor crying nor pain any more, for the former things have passed away." —REVELATION 21:1-4.

Selected Bibliography

Beyer, Richard J. *Medjugorje Day By Day*—Notre Dame, Indiana: Ave Maria Press, 1993.

Craig, Mary. *Spark from Heaven*—Notre Dame, Indiana: Ave Maria Press, 1988.

Delaney, John J. (editor). *A Woman Clothed With The Sun*—Garden City, New York: Image Books, 1960.

Sister Emmanuel. *Medjugorje, The 90's*—McKees Rocks, Pennyslvania: St. Andrews Productions, 1997.

Gobbi, Stefano. *To the Priests, Our Lady's Beloved Sons* —St. Francis, Maine: The National Headquarters of the Marian Movement of Priests in the United States of America, 1998.

Manuel, David. *Medjugorje Under Siege*—Brewster, Massachusetts: Paraclete Press, 1992.

Pelletier, Joseph A., A.A. *The Queen of Peace Visits Medjugorje*—Worcester, Massachusetts: Assumption Publications, 1985.

—— *The Sun Danced at Fatima*—Garden City, New York: Image Books, 1983.

—— *Our Lady Comes To Garabandal*—Worcester, Massachusetts: Assumption Publications, 1971.

Petrisko, Thomas W. *The Fatima Prophecies*—McKees Rocks, Pennyslvania: St. Andrews Productions, 1998.

Valtorta, Maria. *Poem of the Man-God, Vol. 1*—Sherbrooke, Quebec, Canada: Central Distributors for Valtorta, 1986.

Weible, Wayne. *Letters From Medjugorje*—Brewster, Massachusetts: Paraclete Press, 1991.

—— *Medjugorje: The Message*—Brewster, Massachusetts: Paraclete Press, 1989.

—— *Medjugorje: The Mission*—Brewster, Massachusetts: Paraclete Press, 1994.

—— *Words From Heaven*—Birmingham, Alabama: Saint James Publishing, 1990.

Index

Here is a list of the monthly messages given to visionary Marija, beginning with January 1987. The monthly messages used in the chapters of the book are not included in the index.

Each monthly message begins with the greeting *Dear children,* and closes with *Thank you for responding to my call,* or a variation of those words. The messages are presented with the greeting and closing only at the beginning and end of each year, thus allowing the messages to be read as direct conversations, with a minimum of interruption.

1987: *"Dear children: Behold, also today I want to call you to start living a new life as of today. Dear children, I want you to comprehend that God has chosen each one of you, in order to use you in a great plan for the salvation of mankind. You are not able to comprehend how great your role is in God's design. Therefore, dear children, pray so that in prayer you may be able to comprehend what God's plan is in your regard. I am with you in order that you* *may be able to bring it about in all its fullness.* (February) *Today, I want to wrap you all in my mantle and lead you all along the way of conversion. Dear children, I beseech you, surrender to the Lord your entire past, all the evil that has accumulated in your hearts. I want each one of you to be happy. Therefore, dear children, pray, and in prayer you shall realize a new way of joy. Joy will manifest in your hearts and thus you shall be joyful witnesses of that which I and my Son want from each one of you. I am blessing you.* (March) *I am grateful to you for your presence in this place, where I am giving you special graces. I call each one of you to begin to live as of today that life which God wishes of you and to begin to perform good works of love and mercy. I do not want you, dear children, to live the message and be committing sin, which is displeasing to me. Therefore, dear children, I want each of you to live a new life without the murder of all that God produces in you and is giving you. I give you my special blessing and I am remaining with you on your way to conversion.* (April) *I am calling you to prayer. You know, dear children, that God grants special graces in prayer. Therefore, seek and pray in order that you may be able to comprehend all that I am giving here. I call you, dear children, to prayer with the heart. You know that without prayer you cannot comprehend all that God is planning through each one of you. Therefore, pray! I desire that through each one of you God's plan may be fulfilled, that all which God has planted in your heart may keep on growing. So pray that God's blessing may protect each one of you from all the evil that is threatening you. I bless you, dear children.* (May) *I am calling every one of you to start living in God's love. Dear children, you are ready to commit sin, and to put yourselves in the hands of Satan without reflecting. I call on each one of you to consciously decide for God and against Satan. I am your mother and, therefore, I want to lead you all to complete holiness. I want each one of you to be happy here on earth and to be with me in Heaven. That is, dear children, the purpose of my coming here and it's my desire.* (June, sixth anniversary of the apparitions) *Today I thank you and I want to invite you all to God's peace. I want each one of you to experience in your heart that peace which God gives. I want to bless you all today. I am blessing you with God's blessing and I beseech you, dear children, to follow and to live my way. I love you, dear children, and so not even counting the number of times, I go on calling you and I thank you for all that you are doing for my intentions. I beg you, help me to present you to God and to save you. (July) I beseech you to take up the way of holiness beginning today. I love you and, therefore, I want you to be holy. I do not want Satan to block you on that way. Dear children, pray and accept all that God is offering you on a way which is bitter. But at the same time, God will reveal every sweetness to whoever begins to go on that way, and He will gladly answer every call of God. Do not attribute importance to petty things. Long for heaven. (August) I am calling you all in order that each one of you decides to live my messages. God has permitted me also in this year, which the Church has dedicated to me, to be able to speak to you and to be able to spur you on to holiness. Dear children, seek from God the graces which He is giving you through me. I am ready to intercede with God for all that you seek so that your holiness may be complete. Therefore, dear children, do not forget to seek, because God has permitted me to obtain graces for you. (September) I want to call you all to prayer. Let prayer be your life. Dear children, dedicate your time only to Jesus and He will give you everything that you are seeking. He will reveal Himself to you in fullness. Dear children, Satan is strong and is waiting to test each one of you. Pray, and that way he will neither be able to injure you nor block you on the way to holiness. Dear children, through prayer grow all the more toward God from day to day. (October) I want to call all of you to decide for Paradise. The way is difficult for those who have not decided for God. Dear children, decide and believe that God is offering Himself to you in His fullness. You are invited and you need to answer the call of the Father, who is calling you through me. Pray, because in prayer each one of you will be able to achieve complete love. I am blessing you and I desire to help you so that each one of you might be under my motherly mantle. (November) I call each one of you to decide to surrender again everything completely to me. Only that way will I be able to present each of you to God. Dear children, you know that I love you immeasurably and that I desire each of you for myself, but God has given to all a freedom which I lovingly respect and humbly submit to. I desire, dear children, that you help so that everything God has planned in this parish shall be realized. If you do not pray, you shall not be able to recognize my love and the plans which God has for this parish and for each individual. Pray that Satan does not entice you with his pride and deceptive strength. I am with you and I want you to believe me, that I love you.* (Christmas Day) *Rejoice with me! My heart is rejoicing because of Jesus and today I want to give Him to you. Dear children, I want each one of you to open your heart to Jesus and I will give Him to you with love. Dear children, I want Him to change you, to teach you, and to protect you. Today I am praying in a special way for each one of you and I am presenting you to God so He will manifest Himself in you. I am calling you to sincere prayer with the heart so that every prayer of yours may be an encounter with God. In your work, and in your everyday life, put God in the first place. I call you today with great seriousness to obey me and to do as I am calling you. Thank you for responding to my call."*

1988: *"Dear children: Today again I am calling you to complete conversion, which is difficult for those who have not chosen God. I am calling you, dear children, to convert fully to God. God can give you everything that you seek from Him. But you seek God only when sickness, problems, and difficulties come to you and you think that God is far from you and is not listening and does not hear your prayers. No, dear children, that is not the truth! When you are far from God, you cannot receive graces because you do not seek them with a firm faith. Day by day, I am praying for you and I want to draw you ever closer to God; but I cannot if you don't want it. Therefore, dear children, put your life in God's hands.* (February) *Today again I am calling you to prayer and complete surrender to God. You know that I love you and am* coming here out of love, so I could show you the path of peace and salvation for your souls. I want you to obey me and not permit Satan to seduce you. Dear children, Satan is very strong and, therefore, I ask you to dedicate your prayers to me so that those who are under his influence may be saved. Give witness by your life, sacrifice your lives for the salvation of the world. I am with you and I am grateful to you, but in heaven you shall receive the Father's reward which He has promised you. Therefore, little children, do not be afraid. If you pray, Satan cannot injure you even a little, because you are God's children and He is watching over you. Pray, and let the Rosary always be in your hands as a sign to Satan that you belong to me. (March) I am calling you to a complete surrender to God. You, dear children, are not conscious of how God loves you with such a great love. Because of it He permits me to be with you so I can instruct you and help you to find the way of peace. That way, however, you cannot discover if you do not pray. Therefore, dear children, forsake everything and consecrate your time to God and then God will bestow gifts upon you and bless you. Little children, do not forget that your life is fleeting like the spring flower which today is wondrously beautiful, but tomorrow has vanished. Therefore, pray in such a way that your prayer, your surrender to God may become like a road sign. That way, your witness will not only have value for yourselves, but for all of eternity. (April) God wants to make you holy. Therefore, through me He is calling you to complete surrender. Let the Holy Mass be your life. Understand that the church is God's palace, the place in which I gather you and want to show you the way of God. Come and pray! Neither look to others nor slander them, but rather let your life be a testimony on the way of holiness. Churches deserve respect and are set apart as holy because God, who became Man, dwells in them day and night. Therefore, little children, believe and pray that the Father increases your faith, and then ask for whatever you need. I am with you and I rejoice because of your conversion and I am protecting you with my motherly mantle. (May) I am calling you to a complete surrender to God. Pray, little chil-

dren, that Satan does not sway you like branches in the wind. Be strong in God. I desire that through you the whole world may get to know the God of joy. Neither be anxious or worried. God will help you and show you the way. I want you to love all men with my love, both the good and the bad. Only that way will love conquer the world. Little children, you are mine. I love you and I want you to surrender to me so I can lead you to God. Pray without ceasing so that Satan cannot take advantage of you. Pray so that you realize that you are mine. I bless you with the blessing of joy. (June, seventh anniversary) *I am calling you to the love which is loyal and pleasing to God. Little children, love bears everything bitter and difficult for the sake of Jesus, who is love. Therefore, dear children, pray God to come to your aid, not, however, according to your desires but according to His love. Surrender yourselves to God so that He may heal you, console you, and forgive everything inside you which is a hindrance on the way of love. In this way, God can mold your life and you will grow in love. Dear children, glorify God with the canticle of love so that God's love may be able to grow in you day by day to its fullness.* (July) *I am calling you to a complete surrender to God. Everything you do and everything that you possess give over to God so that He can take control in your life as King of all that you possess. That way, through me God can lead you into the depths of the spiritual life. Little children, do not be afraid because I am with you even when you think there is no way out and that Satan is in control. I am bringing peace to you. I am your Mother and the Queen of Peace. I am blessing you with the blessing of joy so that for you God may be everything in life.* (August) *I invite you all to rejoice in the life which God gives you. Little children, rejoice in God the Creator because He has created you so wonderfully. Pray that your life be a joyful thanksgiving, which flows out of your heart like a river of joy. Little children, give thanks unceasingly for all that you possess, for each little gift, which God has given you so that a joyful blessing always comes down from God upon your life.* (September) *I am calling all of you without exception to the way of holi-*

ness in your life. God gave you the gift of holiness. Pray that you may more and more comprehend it and in that way, you will be able by your life to bear witness for God. Dear children, I am blessing you and I intercede for you to God so that your way and your witness may be a complete one and a joy for God. (October) My call that you live the messages which I am giving you is a daily one, especially, little children, because I want to draw you closer to the Heart of Jesus. Therefore, little children, I am calling you today to the prayer of Consecration to Jesus, my dear Son, so that each of your hearts may be His. And then I am calling you to Consecration to my Immaculate Heart. I want you to consecrate yourselves as persons, families, and parishes so that all belongs to God through my hands. Therefore, little children, pray that you may comprehend the greatness of this message which I am giving you. I do not want anything for myself, rather, all for the salvation of your souls. Satan is strong and, therefore, you, little children, by constant prayer press tightly to my motherly heart. (November) I am calling you to prayer so that in prayer you have an encounter with God. God is offering and giving Himself to you. But He seeks from you that you answer His call in your freedom. Therefore, little children, set a time during the day when you can pray in peace and humility and meet with God the Creator. I am with you and I intercede with God for you. So be on watch that every encounter in prayer be a joyful meeting with God. Thank you for responding to my call."

1989: "Dear children, today, I am calling you to the way of holiness. Pray that you may comprehend the beauty and the greatness of this way, where God reveals Himself to you in a special way. Pray that you may be open to everything that God is doing through you and that in your life you may be enabled to give thanks to God and to rejoice over everything that He is doing through each individual. I am giving you my blessing. (February) I am calling you to prayer of the heart. Throughout this season of grace, I desire each of you to be united with Jesus; but without *unceasing prayer, you cannot experience the beauty and greatness of the grace which God is offering you. Therefore, little children, at all times fill your heart with even the smallest prayers. I am with you and unceasingly I keep watch over every heart which is given to me. (March) I am calling you to a complete surrender to God. I am calling you to great joy and peace which only God can give. I am with you and I intercede for you everyday before God. I call you, little children, to listen to me and to live the messages which I am giving you. For years you have been invited to holiness, but you are still far away. I am blessing you. (April) I am calling you to a complete surrender to God. Let everything that you possess be in the hands of God. Only in that way shall you have joy in your heart. Little children, rejoice in everything that you have and give thanks to God because everything is God's gift to you. That way in your life you should be able to give thanks for everything and discover God in everything, even in the smallest flower. (May) I am calling you to openness to God. You see, little children, how nature is opening herself and is giving life and fruits. In the same way I am calling you to a life with God and a complete surrender to Him. Little children, I am with you and unceasingly I desire to lead you into the joy of life. I desire that each one of you discovers the joy and the love which is found only in God and which only God can give. God wants nothing else from you but your surrender. Therefore, little children, decide seriously for God because everything passes away. God alone does not pass away. Pray that you may discover the greatness and the joy of life which God is giving you. (July) I am calling you to renew your heart. Open yourself to God and surrender to Him all your difficulties and crosses so God may turn everything into joy. Little children, you cannot open yourselves to God if you do not pray; therefore, from today decide to consecrate a time and a day only for an encounter with God in silence. In that way you will be able, with God, to witness my presence here. Little children, I do not wish to force you; rather, freely give God your time, like children of God. (August) I call you to prayer. By means of prayer, little children, you will obtain joy and peace. Through prayer you are richer in the mercy of God. Therefore, little children, let prayer be the light for each one of you. Especially, I call you to pray so that all those who are far from God may be converted. Then our hearts shall be richer because God will rule in the hearts of all men. Therefore, little children, pray, pray, pray. Let prayer begin to rule in the whole world.* (September) *Today I invite you to give thanks to God for all the gifts you have discovered in the course of your life and even for the least gift you have received. I give thanks with you and want all of you to experience the joy of these gifts, and I want God to be everything for each one of you. And then, little children, you can grow continuously on the way of holiness.* (October) *I am inviting you to prayer. I am always inviting you, but you are still far away. Therefore, from today, decide seriously to dedicate time to God. I am with you and I wish to teach you to pray with the heart. In prayer with the heart, you shall encounter God. Therefore, dear children, pray, pray, pray!* (November) *I have been inviting you for years by these messages which I am giving you. Little children, by means of the messages I wish to make a very beautiful mosaic in your heart so I may be able to present each one of you to God like the original image. Therefore, little children, I desire that your decisions be free before God, because He has given you freedom. Therefore, pray so that, free from any influence of Satan, you may decide only for God. I am praying for you before God and I am seeking your surrender to God.* (Christmas Day) *Today I bless you in a special way with my Motherly blessing and I intercede for you to God for Him to give you the gift of the conversion of the heart. For years I have been calling you to encourage you to a profound spiritual life in simplicity, but you are so cold! Therefore, little children, accept with seriousness and live the messages for your soul not to be sad when I will not be with you anymore and when I will not guide you anymore like an insecure child in his first steps. Therefore, little children, read every day the messages I gave you and transform them into life. I love you and this is why I call you to the way of salvation. Thank you for your response to my call."*

1990: *"Dear children, (February) I invite you to surrender to God. In this season (Lent), I want you to renounce all the things to which you are attached but that hurt your spiritual life. Therefore, little children, decide completely for God, and do not allow Satan to come into your life through those things that hurt both you and your spiritual life. Little children, God is offering Himself to you in fullness and you can discover and recognize Him only in prayer. Make a decision for prayer. (April) Today I invite you to accept with seriousness and to live the messages which I am giving you. I am with you and I desire, dear children, that each of you be ever closer to my heart. Therefore, little children, pray and seek the will of God in your everyday life. I desire that each one of you discover the way of holiness and grow in it until eternity. I will pray for you and intercede for you before God that you receive the greatness of this gift, which God is giving me that I can be with you. (May) I invite you to decide with seriousness to live this Novena (for Pentecost). Consecrate the time to prayer and to sacrifice. I am with you and I desire to help you grow in renunciation and mortification that you may be able to understand the beauty of the lives of people who go on giving themselves to me in a special way. Dear children, God blesses you day after day and desires a change of your life. (June, ninth anniversary) I desire to thank you for all your sacrifices and for all your prayers. I am blessing you with my special Motherly blessing. I invite you all to decide for God so that, from day to day, you will discover His will in prayer. I desire, dear children, to call all of you to a full conversion so that joy will be in your hearts. I am happy that you are here today in such great numbers. (July) I invite you to peace. I have come here as the Queen of Peace and I desire to enrich you with my Motherly Peace. Dear children, I love you and I desire to bring all of you to the peace which only God gives and which enriches every heart. I invite you to become carriers and witnesses of my peace to this unpeaceful world. Let peace rule in the whole world,* *which is without peace and longs for peace. I bless you with my Motherly Blessing.* (August) *I invite you to take with seriousness and put into practice the messages, which I am giving you. You know, little children, that I am with you and I desire to lead you along the same path to Heaven, which is beautiful for those who discover it in prayer. Therefore, little children, do not forget that these messages I am giving you have to be put into your everyday life in order that you might be able to say, 'There, I have taken the messages and tried to live them.' Dear children, I am protecting you before the Heavenly Father by my own prayers.* (September) *I invite you to pray with the heart in order that your prayer may be a conversation with God. I desire that each of you dedicate more time to God. Satan is strong and wants to destroy and deceive you in many ways. Therefore, dear children, pray every day that your life will be good for yourself and all those in need. I am with you and I am protecting you even though Satan wishes to destroy my plan and to hinder the desires which the Heavenly Father wants to realize here.* (October) *I call you to pray in a special way, that you offer up sacrifices and good deeds for peace in the world. Satan is strong and, with all his strength, tries to destroy the peace which comes from God. Therefore, dear children, pray in a special way with me for peace. I am with you and I desire to help you with my prayers and I desire to guide you on the path of peace. I bless you with my Motherly Blessing. Do not forget to live the messages of peace.* (November) *I invite you to do works of mercy with love and out of love for me and your brothers and sisters. Dear children, all that you do for others do with great joy and humility toward God. I am with you and, day after day, I offer your sacrifices and prayers to God for the salvation of the world.* (Christmas Day) *I invite you, in a special way, to pray for peace. Dear children, without peace, you cannot experience the birth of the Child Jesus today or in your daily lives. Therefore, pray that the Lord of Peace may protect you with His Mantle and that He help you to comprehend the greatness and the importance of peace in your hearts. In this way, you shall be able to spread peace from your hearts throughout the whole world. I am with you and I intercede for you before God. Pray, because Satan wants to destroy my plan of peace. Be reconciled with one another and, by means of your lives, work that peace may reign in the whole world. Thank you for your response to my call."*

1991: *"Dear children, today, like never before, I invite you to prayer. Your prayer should be a prayer for peace. Satan is strong and wishes not only to destroy human life, but also nature and the planet on which we live. Therefore, dear children, pray that you can protect yourselves, through prayer, with the blessing of God's peace. God sends me to you so that I can help you if you wish to accept the rosary. Even the rosary alone can work miracles in the world and in your lives. I bless you and I stay among you as long as it is God's will. Thank you for not betraying my presence here, and I thank you because your response is serving God and peace. (February) I invite you to decide for God because distance from God is the fruit of the lack of peace in your hearts. God alone is peace. Therefore, approach Him through your personal prayer and then live peace in your hearts. In this way, peace will flow like a river into the whole world. Do not speak about peace, but make peace. I am blessing each of you and each good decision of yours. (April) I invite you so that your prayer be prayer with the heart. Let each of you find time for prayer so that in your prayer you discover God. I do not desire you to talk about prayer, but to pray. Let every day be filled with prayer of gratitude to God for life and for all that you have. I do not desire your life to pass by in words, but that you glorify God with deeds. I am with you, I am grateful to God for every moment spent with you. (May) I invite all of you who have heard my message of peace to realize it with seriousness and with love in your life. There are many who think they are doing a lot by talking about the messages but do not live them. Dear children, I invite you to life and to change all the negative in you so that it all turns into the positive, and into life. Dear children, I am with you and I desire to help each of you to live and,* *by living, to witness to the good news. I am here, dear children, to help you and to lead you to heaven. In heaven is the joy through which you can already live heaven now.* (June, tenth anniversary) *Today, on this great day which you have given me, I desire to bless all of you and to say, 'These days while I am with you are days of grace.' I desire to teach you and to help you walk on the path of holiness. There are many people who do not desire to understand my message and to accept with seriousness what I am saying. But you, I therefore call and ask that, by your life and your daily living, you witness my presence. If you pray, God will help you discover the true reason for my coming. Therefore, little children, pray and read the Sacred Scriptures so that, through my coming, you may discover the message in Sacred Scripture for you.* (July) *Today I invite you to pray for peace. At this time, peace is threatened in a special way and I am seeking from you to renew fasting and prayer in your families. Dear children, I desire you to grasp the seriousness of the situation and that much of what will happen depends on your prayers; and you are praying a little bit. Dear children, I am with you and I am inviting you to begin to pray and fast seriously, as in the first days of my coming.* (August) *I invite you to prayer, now as never before, when my plan has begun to be realized. Satan is strong and wants to sweep away plans of peace and joy and make you think that my Son is not strong in His decisions. Therefore, I call all of you, dear children, to pray and fast still more firmly. I invite you to renunciation for nine days, so that, with your help, everything that I wanted to realize through the secrets which began at Fatima may be fulfilled. I call you, dear children, to grasp the importance of my coming and the seriousness of the situation. I want to save all souls and present them to God. Therefore, let us pray that everything I have begun will be fully realized.* (September) *Today, in a special way, I invite you all to prayer and renunciation. For now, as never before, Satan wants to show the world his shameful face, by which he wants to seduce as many people as possible onto the way of death and sin. Therefore, dear children, help my Immaculate Heart to triumph in the sinful world. I beseech all of you to offer prayers and sacrifices for my intentions so I can present them to God for what is most necessary. Forget your desires, dear children, and pray for what God desires and not for what you desire."* (On October 25, the Virgin gave an unusually strong message, indicating the fierceness of the horrific war now engulfing all the areas surrounding Medjugorje. She did not begin with the usual greeting of "Dear children." She only spoke three words and those with great urgency: *"PRAY! PRAY! PRAY!"* Marija stated that the Blessed Virgin also did not give her usual "Thank you for having responded to my call." The messages resumed in their normal state with the November 25 message: *"This time, also, I am inviting you to prayer. Pray that you might be able to comprehend what God desires to tell you through my presence and through the messages I am giving you. I desire to draw you ever closer to Jesus and His wounded heart, that you might be able to comprehend the immeasurable love which gave itself for each one of you. Therefore, dear children, pray that from your heart would flow a fountain of love to every person, both to the one that hates you and to the one that despises you. That way, you will be able, through Jesus' love, to overcome all the misery in this world of sorrow, which is without hope for those who do not know Jesus. I am with you and I love you with the immeasurable love of Jesus. Thank you for all your sacrifices and prayers. Pray so that I might be able to help you still more. Your prayers are necessary to me.* (Christmas Day) *Today, in a special way, I bring the little Jesus to you that He may bless you with His blessings of peace and love. Dear children, do not forget that this is a grace which many people neither understand nor accept. Therefore, you who have said that you are mine and seek my help, give all of yourself. First of all, give your love and example in your families. You say that Christmas is a family feast; therefore, dear children, put God in the first place in your families so that He may give you peace and may protect you not only from war, but also protect you from every Satanic attack during peace. When God is with you, you have everything; but when you do not want Him, then you are miserable and lost and you do not know on whose side you are. Therefore, dear children, decide for God and then you will get everything. Thank you for your response to my call."*

1992: *"Dear children, (April) today also I invite you for prayer. Only by prayer and fasting can war be stopped. Therefore, my dear little children, pray and by your life give witness that you are mine and that you belong to me, because Satan wishes in these turbulent days to seduce as many souls as possible. Therefore, I invite you to decide for God and He will protect you and show you what you should do and which path to take. I invite all those who have said yes to me to renew their consecration to my Son, Jesus, and to His heart and to me so we can take you more intensely as instruments of peace in this unpeaceful world. Medjugorje is a sign to all of you and a call to pray and live the days of grace that God is giving you. Therefore, little children, accept the call to prayer with seriousness. I am with you and your suffering is also mine. (May) I invite you to prayer so that through prayer you come yet closer to God. I am with you and I wish to lead you on the path of salvation which Jesus gives. From day to day I am closer and closer to you although you are not conscious of it and do not want to admit that you are connected to me in prayer only a little bit. When temptations and problems arise, you say, 'Oh God, oh Mother, where are you?' And I only wait for you to accept my call and begin anew to pray, until prayer becomes joy for you, and then you will discover that God is Almighty in your everyday life. I am with you and I wait for you. (June, eleventh anniversary) I am happy despite there still being some sadness in my heart for all those who began to take this path and then abandoned it. My presence here is therefore to lead you on a new path, the path of salvation. Thus, I call you day after day to conversion, but if you do not pray, you cannot say you are converting. I pray for you and intercede before God for peace. First, for peace in your heart, then around you, so that God may be your peace. (July) Today again, I invite all of you to prayer, so that in these sad days, none of you* *feels sadness in prayer, but a joyful meeting with God, your creator. Pray little children, so that you can be closer to me and feel through prayer what I desire from you. I am with you and every day I bless you with my motherly blessing, so that the Lord may bestow you with the abundance of His grace for your daily life. Thank God for the gift of my being with you because I am telling you, this is a great grace.* (August) *I wish to tell you that I love you with my motherly love, and I call upon you to open yourselves completely to me so that through each of you, I may be enabled to convert and save the world, where there is much sin and many that are evil. Therefore, my dear children, open yourselves completely to me so that I may be able to lead you more and more to the marvelous love of God the Creator, who reveals Himself to you day by day. I am at your side and I wish to reveal to you and to show you the God who loves you.* (September) *Today also, I wish to tell you I am with you in these restless days in which Satan wishes to destroy everything I and my Son, Jesus, are building up. In a special way he wishes to destroy your souls. He wishes to guide you as far as possible from the Christian life, as well as from the Commandments to which the Church is calling you so you may live them. Satan wishes to destroy everything which is holy in you and around you. Therefore little children, pray, pray, pray in order to be able to comprehend all which God is giving you through my coming.* (October) *I invite you to prayer now, when Satan is strong and wishes to make as many souls as possible his own. Pray, dear children, and have more trust in me because I am here in order to help you and to guide you on a new path towards a new life. Therefore, dear little children, listen and live what I tell you because it is important for you when I shall not be with you any longer that you remember my words and all which I told you. I call you to change your life from the beginning and that you decide for conversion, not with words but with your life.* (November) *Today, like never before, I invite you to pray. May your life become prayer in fullness. Without love you cannot pray. Therefore, I invite you to first love God the creator of your life, and then you shall also discover and love God in all as He loves you. Dear children, it is a grace that I am with you. Therefore, accept and live my messages for your good. I love you and therefore, I am with you to teach you and to guide you to a new life of renunciation and conversion. Only in this way you shall discover God and everything which is far from you now. Therefore, little children, pray.* (Christmas Day) *I wish to place you all under my mantle to protect you from every satanic attack. Today is the Day of Peace, but throughout the whole world there is much lack of peace. Therefore, I call you to build up a new world of peace together with me by means of prayer. Without you, I cannot do that and therefore, I call all of you with my motherly love and God will do the rest. Therefore, open yourselves to God's plans and purposes for you to be able to cooperate with Him for peace and for good. And, do not forget that your life does not belong to you, but is a gift with which you must bring joy to others and lead them to eternal life. May the tenderness of my little Jesus always accompany you. Thank you for your response to my call."*

1993: *"Dear children, (April) I invite you all to awaken your hearts to love. Go into nature and look how nature is awakening and it will be a help for you to open your hearts to the love of God the Creator. I desire you to awaken love in your families so that where there is unrest and hatred, love will reign and when there is love in your hearts there is also prayer. And, dear children, do not forget that I am with you and I am helping you with my prayer that God may give you the strength to love. I bless and love you with my Motherly love. (May) I invite you to open yourselves to God by means of prayer so the Holy Spirit may begin to work miracles in you and through you. I am with you and I intercede before God for each one of you because, dear children, each one of you is important in my plan of salvation. I invite you to be carriers of good and peace. God can give you peace only if you convert and pray. Therefore, my dear little children, Pray! Pray! Pray! And do that which the Holy Spirit inspires you to do. (July) I invite you to* *pray for peace. At this time, peace is threatened in a special way; and I am seeking from you to renew fasting and prayer in your families. Dear children, I desire for you to grasp the seriousness of the situation and that much of what will happen depends on your prayers, and you are praying a little bit. Dear children, I am with you and I am inviting you to begin to pray and fast seriously, as in the first days of my coming.* (August) *I want you to understand that I am your Mother, that I want to help you and call you to prayer. Only by prayer can you understand and accept my messages and practice them in your life. Read Sacred Scripture, live it, and pray to understand the signs of the time. This is a special time. Therefore, I am with you to draw you close to my heart and the Heart of my Son, Jesus. Dear little children, I want you to be children of the light and not of darkness. Therefore, live what I am telling you.* (September) *I am your Mother and I invite you to come closer to God through prayer, because only He is your peace, your Savior. Therefore, little children, do not seek comfort in material things; rather, seek God. I am praying for you and I intercede before God for each individual. I am looking for your prayers, that you accept me and accept my messages as in the first days of the apparitions. And only then, when you open your hearts and pray, will miracles happen.* (October) *I have been calling you to pray, to live what I am telling you, but you are living my messages a little. You talk but do not live. That is why, my dear little children, this war is lasting so long. I invite you to open yourselves to God and to live with God in your hearts, living the good and giving witness to my messages. I love you and wish to protect you from every evil, but you do not desire it. Dear children, I cannot help you if you do not live God's Commandments, if you do not live the Mass, if you do not abandon sin. I invite you to become Apostles of Love and Goodness. In this world without peace, give witness to God and God's love and God will bless you and give you what you seek of Him.* (November) *I invite you now, in this time, like never before, to prepare for the coming of Jesus. Let little Jesus reign in your hearts; and only then, when Jesus is your friend, will you be happy. It will not be difficult for you either to pray or offer sacrifices or to witness Jesus' greatness in your life, because He will give you strength and joy in this time. I am close to you by my intercession and prayer and I love and bless all of you.* (Christmas Day) *Today I rejoice with the little Jesus and I desire that Jesus' joy may enter into every heart. Little children, with the message I give you a blessing with my Son, Jesus, so that in every heart peace may reign. I love you, little children, and I invite all of you to come closer to me by means of prayer. You talk and talk but do not pray. Therefore, little children, decide for prayer. Only in this way will you be happy and God will give you what you seek from Him. Thank you for your response to my call."*

1994: *"Dear children, (March) I rejoice with you and I invite you to open yourselves to me and become an instrument in my hands, for the salvation of the world. I desire, little children, that all of you who have felt the fragrance of holiness, through these messages which I am giving you, to carry it in this world, hungry for God and God's love. I thank you all for having responded in such a number and I bless you all with my motherly blessing. (April) I invite all of you to decide to pray for my intention. Little children, I invite all of you to help me realize my plan through this parish. Now, in a special way, little children, I invite you to decide to go the way of holiness. Only then will you be close to me. I love you and want to lead you all with me to paradise. But, if you do not pray and if you are not humble and obedient to the messages I am giving you, I cannot help you. (May) I invite all of you to have more trust in me and to live my messages more deeply. I am with you and intercede before God for you, but also I wait for your hearts to open up to my messages. Rejoice because God loves you and gives you the possibility to convert every day and to believe more in God, the Creator. (July) I invite you to decide to give time to prayer patiently. Little children, you cannot say you are mine and that you have experienced conversion through my messages if you are not ready to give time to God every day. I am* *close to you and I bless you all. Little children, do not forget that if you do not pray, you are not close to me nor are you close to the Holy Spirit, who leads you along the path to holiness. (August) I am united with you in prayer in a special way, praying for the gift of the presence of my Beloved Son* (Our Lady is referring to the Pope) *in your home country. Pray, little children, for the health of my most beloved son, who suffers and whom I have chosen for these times. I pray and intercede before my Son, Jesus, so that the dream that your fathers had may be fulfilled. Pray, little children, in a special way because Satan is strong and wants to destroy hope in your heart. I bless you. (September) I rejoice with you and I invite you to prayer. Little children, pray for my intention. Your prayers are necessary to me, through which I desire to bring you closer to God. He is your salvation. God sends me to help you and to guide you towards Paradise, which is your goal. Therefore, little children, Pray! Pray! Pray! (October) I am with you and I rejoice today because the Most High has granted me to be with you and to teach you and to guide you on the path of perfection. Little children, I wish you to be a beautiful bouquet of flowers which I wish to present to God for the day of All Saints. I invite you to open yourselves and to live, taking the saints as an example. Mother church has chosen them, that they may be an impulse for your daily life. (November) I call you to prayer. I am with you all. I am your mother and I wish that your hearts be similar to my heart. Little children, without prayer you cannot live and say that you are mine. Prayer is a joy. Prayer is what the human heart desires. Therefore, get closer, little children, to my Immaculate Heart and you will discover God. Thank you for your response to my call."*

1995: *"Dear children, I invite you to open the door of your heart to Jesus as the flower opens itself to the sun. Jesus desires to fill your hearts with peace and joy. You cannot, little children, realize peace if you are not at peace with Jesus. Therefore, I invite you to confession so Jesus may be your truth and peace. So, little chil-*

dren, pray to have the strength to realize what I am telling you. I am with you and I love you. (March) I invite you to live peace in your hearts and families. There is no peace, little children, where there is no prayer; and there is no love where there is no faith. Therefore, little children, I invite you all to decide again today for conversion. I am close to you and I invite you all, little children, into my embrace to help you. But you do not want it; so Satan is tempting you, and in the smallest things your faith disappears. This is why, dear children, pray; and through prayer, you will have blessing and peace. (May) I invite you, little children, to help me through your prayers so that as many hearts as possible come close to my Immaculate Heart. Satan is strong and with all his forces wants to bring the most people possible closer to himself and to sin, that is why he is on the prowl to snatch more every moment. I beg you, little children, pray and help me to help you. I am your Mother and I love you and that is why I wish to help you. (June, fourteenth anniversary) Today I am happy to see you in such great numbers that you have responded and have come to live my messages. I invite you, little children, to be my joyful carrier of peace in this troubled world. Pray for peace so that as soon as possible a time of peace which my heart waits impatiently for my reign. I am near you, little children, and I intercede for every one of you before the Most High. I bless you with my Motherly blessing. (July) I invite you to prayer because only in prayer can you understand my coming here. The Holy Spirit will enlighten you to understand that you must convert, little children. I wish to make of you a most beautiful bouquet prepared for eternity but you do not accept the way of conversion, the way of salvation that I am offering you through these apparitions. Little children, pray, convert your hearts and come closer to me. May good overcome evil. I love you and bless you. (August) Today, I invite you to prayer. Let prayer be life for you. A family cannot say that it is in peace if it does not pray. Therefore, let your morning begin with morning prayer and your evening end with thanksgiving. Little children, I am with you and I love you. I bless you and I wish for everyone of you to be in *my embrace. You cannot be in my embrace if you are not ready to pray every day.* (September) *I invite you to fall in love with the most Holy Sacrament of the Altar. Adore Him, little children, in your parishes, and in this way you will be united with the entire world. Jesus will become your friend and you will not talk of Him like someone whom you barely know. Unity with Him will be a joy for you and you will become witnesses to the love of Jesus that He has for every creature. When you adore Jesus, you are also close to me.* (October) *Today I invite you to go into nature because there you will meet God the Creator. Today, I invite you, little children, to thank God for all that He gives you. In thanking Him, you will discover the Most High and all the goods that surround you. Little children, God is great and His love for every creature is great. Therefore, pray to be able to understand the love and goodness of God. In the goodness and the love of God, the Creator, I am also with you as a gift.* (November) *I invite you that each of you begin again to love—in the first place—God, who saved and redeemed each of you, and then brothers and sisters in your proximity. Without love, little children, you cannot grow in holiness and cannot do good deeds. Therefore, little children, pray without ceasing that God reveals His love to you. I have invited all of you to unite yourselves with me and to love. Today, I am with you and I invite you to discover love in your hearts and in the families. For God to live in your hearts, you must love.* (Christmas Day) *Today, I also rejoice with you and I bring you little Jesus, so that He may bless you. I invite you, dear children, so that your life may be united with Him. Jesus is the King of Peace and only He can give you the peace that you seek. I am with you and I present you to Jesus in a special way, now in this new time in which one should decide for Him. This time is the time of grace. Thank you for your response to my call."*

1996: *"Dear Children, today I invite you to decide for peace. Pray to God that He will give you true peace. Live peace in your hearts and you will understand, dear children, that peace is God's* *gift. Dear children, without love you cannot live peace. The fruit of peace is love and the fruit of love is forgiveness. I am with you and I am inviting all of you, little children, to first forgive in the family and then you will be able to forgive others.* (February) *Today, I invite you to conversion. This is the most important message that I have given you here. Little children, I wish that each of you become a carrier of my messages. I invite you, little children, to live the messages that I have given you over these years. This is a time of grace, especially now when the church also is inviting you to prayer and conversion. I also, little children, invite you to live my messages that I have given you during the time since I appeared here.* (April) *I invite you again to put prayer in the first place in your families. Little children, when God is in the first place, then you will, in all that you do, seek the will of God. In this way your daily conversion will become easier. Little children, seek with humility that which is not in order in your hearts, and you shall understand what you have to do. Conversion will become a daily duty that you will do with joy. Little children, I am with you, I bless you all and I invite you to become my witnesses by prayer and personal conversion.* (May) *Today I wish to thank you for all your prayers and sacrifices that you, during this month which is dedicated to me, have offered to me. Little children, I also wish that you all become active during this time, that is through me connected to heaven in a special way. Pray in order to understand that you all, through your life and your example, ought to collaborate in the work of salvation. Little children, I wish that all people convert and see me and my Son, Jesus, in you. I will intercede for you and help you to become the light. In helping the other, your soul will also find salvation.* (June, fifteenth anniversary) *I thank you for all the sacrifices you have offered me these days. Little children, I invite you to open yourselves to me and to decide for conversion. Your hearts, little children, are still not completely open to me and therefore, I invite you again to open to prayer so that in prayer the Holy Spirit will help you, that your hearts become of flesh and not of stone. Little children, thank you for having responded to my call and for having decided to walk with me toward holiness.* (July) *Today I invite you to decide every day for God. Little children, you speak much about God, but you witness little with your life. Therefore, little children, decide for conversion, that your life may be true before God, so that in the truth of your life you witness the beauty God gave you. Little children, I invite you again to decide for prayer because through prayer, you will be able to live the conversion. Each one of you shall become in the simplicity, similar to a child, which is open to the love of the Father.* (August) *Listen, because I wish to speak to you and to invite you to have more faith and trust in God, who loves you immeasurably. Little children, you do not know how to live in the grace of God, that is why I call you all anew, to carry the word of God in your heart and in your thoughts. Little children, place the Sacred Scripture in a visible place in your family, and read and live it. Teach your children, because if you are not an example to them, children depart into godlessness. Reflect and pray and then God will be born in your heart and your heart will be joyous.* (September) *Today I invite you to offer your crosses and suffering for my intentions. Little children, I am your mother and I wish to help you by seeking for you the grace from God. Little children, offer your sufferings as a gift to God so they become a most beautiful flower of joy. That is why, little children, pray that you may understand that suffering can become joy and the cross the way of joy.* (October) *I invite you to open yourselves to God the Creator, so that He changes you. Little children, you are dear to me. I love you all and I call you to be closer to me and that your love towards my Immaculate Heart be more fervent. I wish to renew you and lead you with my Heart to the Heart of Jesus, which still today suffers for you and calls you to conversion and renewal. Through you, I wish to renew the world. Comprehend, little children, that you are today the salt of the earth and the light of the world. Little children, I invite you and I love you and in a special way implore: Convert!* (November) *Today, again, I invite you to pray, so that through prayer, fasting and small sacrifices you may prepare yourselves for the coming of*

Jesus. May this time, little children, be a time of grace for you. Use every moment and do good, for only in this way will you feel the birth of Jesus in your hearts. If with your life you give an example and become a sign of God's love, joy will prevail in the hearts of men. (Christmas Day) *I am with you in a special way, holding little Jesus in my lap, and I invite you, little children, to open yourselves to His call. He calls you to joy. Little children, joyfully live the messages of the Gospel, which I am repeating in the time since I am with you. Little children, I am your Mother and I desire to reveal to you the God of love and the God of peace. I do not desire for your life to be in sadness but that it be realized in joy for eternity, according to the Gospel. Only in this way will your life have meaning. Thank you for having responded to my call"*

1997: *"Dear children! I invite you to reflect about your future. You are creating a new world without God, only with your own strength and that is why you are unsatisfied and without joy in the heart. This time is my time and that is why, little children, I invite you again to pray. When you find unity with God, you will feel hunger for the word of God and your heart, little children, will overflow with joy. You will witness God's love wherever you are. I bless you and I repeat to you that I am with you to help you.* (February) *Today I invite you in a special way to open yourselves to God the Creator and to become active. I invite you, little children, to see at this time who needs your spiritual or material help. By your example, little children, you will be the extended hands of God, which humanity is seeking. Only in this way will you understand that you are called to witness and to become joyful carriers of God's word and of His love.* (April) *Today I call you to have your life be connected with God the Creator, because only in this way will your life have meaning and you will comprehend that God is love. God sends me to you out of love, that I may help you to comprehend that without Him there is no future or joy and, above all, there is no eternal salvation. Little children, I call you to leave sin and to accept prayer at all times, that you may in prayer* come to know the meaning of your life. God gives Himself to him who seeks Him. (May) *Today, I invite you to glorify God and for the name of God to be holy in your hearts and in your life. Little children, when you are in the holiness of God, He is with you and gives you peace and joy which come only from God through prayer. That is why, little children, renew prayer in your families and your heart will glorify the holy name of God, and heaven will reign in your heart. I am close to you and I intercede for you before God.* (July) *I invite you to respond to my call to prayer. I desire, dear children, that during this time you find a corner for personal prayer. I desire to lead you towards prayer with the heart. Only in this way will you comprehend that your life is empty without prayer. You will discover the meaning of your life when you discover God in prayer. That is why, little children, open the door of your heart, and you will comprehend that prayer is joy without which you cannot live.* (August) *God gives me this time as a gift to you, so that I may instruct and lead you on the path of salvation. Dear children, now you do not comprehend this grace, but soon a time will come when you will lament for these messages. That is why, little children, live all of the words which I have given you through this time of grace, and renew prayer until prayer becomes a joy for you. Especially, I call all those who have consecrated themselves to my Immaculate Heart to become an example to others. I call all priests and religious brothers and sisters to pray the rosary and to teach others to pray. The rosary, little children, is especially dear to me. Through the rosary open your heart to me and I am able to help you.* (September) *Today I call you to comprehend that without love you cannot comprehend that God needs to be in the first place in your life. That is why, little children, I call you all to love, not with a human but with God's love. In this way, your life will be more beautiful and without an interest. You will comprehend that God gives Himself to you in the simplest way out of love. Little children, so that you may comprehend my words which I give you out of love, pray, pray, pray and you will be able to accept others with love and to forgive all who have done evil to* you. *Respond with prayer; prayer is a fruit of love towards God the Creator.* (November) *Today I invite you to comprehend your Christian vocation. Little children, I led and am leading you through this time of grace, that you may become conscious of your Christian vocation. Holy martyrs died witnessing: I am a Christian and love God over everything. Little children, today also I invite you to rejoice and be joyful Christians, responsible and conscious that God called you in a special way to be joyfully extended hands toward those who do not believe, and that through the example of your life, they may receive faith and love for God. Therefore, pray, pray, pray that your heart may open and be sensitive for the Word of God.* (Christmas Day) *Also today I rejoice with you and I call you to the good. I desire that each of you reflect and carry peace in your heart and say: I want to put God in the first place in my life. In this way, little children, each of you will become holy. Little children, tell everyone, I want the good for you and he will respond with the good and, little children, good will come to dwell in the heart of each man. Little children, tonight I bring to you the good of my Son who gave His life to save you. That is why, little children, rejoice and extend your hands to Jesus who is only good. Thank you for having responded to my call.*"

1998: "*Dear Children! Today again I call all of you to prayer. Only with prayer, dear children, will your heart change, become better, and be more sensitive to the Word of God. Little children, do not permit Satan to pull you apart and to do with you what he wants. I call you to be responsible and determined and to consecrate each day to God in prayer. May Holy Mass, little children, not be a habit for you, but life. By living Holy Mass each day, you will feel the need for holiness and you will grow in holiness. I am close to you and intercede before God for each of you, so that He may give you strength to change your heart.* (February) *Also today I am with you and I, again, call all of you to come closer to me through your prayers. In a special way, I call you to renunciation in this time of grace. Little children, meditate on and live, through your little sacrifices, the passion and death of Jesus for each of you. Through prayer and your renunciation you will become more open to the gift of faith and love towards the Church and the people who are around you. I love you and bless you."* (Mirjana's annual apparition, March 18) The apparition lasted between four and five minutes. Our Lady spoke to her about the secrets, blessed all those present, and gave the following message: *"Dear children! I call you to be my light, in order to enlighten all those who still live in darkness, to fill their hearts with the Peace of my Son. Thank you for having responded to my call!"* (March) *"I call you to fasting and renunciation. Little children, renounce that which hinders you from being closer to Jesus. In a special way I call you: Pray, because only through prayer will you be able to overcome your will and discover the will of God even in the smallest things. By your daily life, little children, you will become an example and witness that you live for Jesus or against Him and His will. Little children, I desire that you become apostles of love. By loving, little children, it will be recognized that you are mine.* (April) *Today again I invite you to open yourselves to God through prayer, as a flower opens to the morning rays of sun. Little children, do not be afraid. I am with you and I intercede for you before the throne of God so that you may receive the gift of conversion. Only in this way will you understand, little children, the importance of grace in these times and God will become dear to you.* (June, seventeenth anniversary) *Today, I desire to thank you for living my messages. I bless you all with my motherly blessing and I bring you all before my Son, Jesus.* (July) *Today, little children, I invite you, through prayer, to be with Jesus, so that through a personal experience of prayer you may be able to discover the beauty of God's creatures. You cannot speak or witness about prayer, if you do not pray. That is why, little children, in the silence of the heart, remain with Jesus, so that He may change and transform you with His love. This, little children, is a time of grace for you. Make good use of it for your personal conversion, because when you have God, you have everything.* (August) *Today I invite you to come still closer to me*

through prayer. Little children, I am your mother, I love you and I
desire that each of you be saved and thus be with me in Heaven.
That is why, little children, pray, pray, pray until your life becomes
prayer. (November) Today I call you to prepare yourselves for the
coming of Jesus. In a special way, prepare your hearts. May holy
Confession be the first act of conversion for you and then, dear
children, decide for holiness. May your conversion and decision
for holiness begin today and not tomorrow. Little children, I call
you all to the way of salvation and I desire to show you the way
to Heaven. That is why, little children, be mine and decide with me
for holiness. Little children, accept prayer with seriousness and
pray, pray, pray. (December) In this Christmas joy I desire to bless
you with my blessing. In a special way, little children, I give you
the blessing of little Jesus. May He fill you with His peace. Today,
little children, you do not have peace and yet you yearn for it. That
is why, with my Son, Jesus, on this day I call you to pray, pray,
pray, because without prayer you do not have joy or peace or a
future. Yearn for peace and seek it, for God is true peace. (First
annual apparition of Jakov) Today, on the birthday of my Son, my
heart is filled with immeasurable joy, love and peace. As your
mother, I desire for each of you to feel that same joy, peace and
love in the heart. That is why do not be afraid to open your heart
and to completely surrender yourself to Jesus, because only in this
way can He enter into your heart and fill it with love, peace and
joy. I bless you with my motherly blessing. Thank you for having
responded to my call."

1999: "Dear children! I again invite you to prayer. You have no
excuse to work more because nature still lies in deep sleep. Open
yourselves in prayer. Renew prayer in your families. Put Holy
Scripture in a visible place in your families, read it, reflect on it and
learn how God loves His people. His love shows itself also in present times because He sends me to call you upon the path of salvation. Thank you for having responded to my call."

These are they who have come out of the great Tribulation; they have washed their robes and made them white in the Blood of the Lamb.

—REVELATION 7:14.

Endnotes

1   The Croatian expression for "Our Lady," an affectionate expression for the Blessed Virgin Mary.

2   Secular priests have no affiliation with a specific order such as the Franciscan or Jesuit orders. Most priests in the Catholic Church are secular priests.

3   I witnessed this phenomenon in May 1986 during my first pilgrimage to Medjugorje. The cross first disappeared as we boarded our bus for Dubrovnik. Ten minutes later as we were driving from the area, it reappeared and began spinning on its axis.

4   This outline is strictly a personal opinion based on early statements given by the visionaries.

5   For an explanation of interior locution, see the description of the locutions received by Jelena Vasilij, on pages 65 and 66.

6   At her apparition in Fatima, the Virgin asked for a special devotion on the first Saturday of the month; this devotion included 15 decades of the rosary, Mass, and confession.

7   Meaning, in apparition.

8   A startling revelation by the Blessed Virgin, and verification that her call for prayer and fasting bears tangible fruits.

9   The Transfiguration of Christ is believed to have taken place on Mount Thabor (or Tabor) in Israel. In this event, three of Jesus' disciples were permitted to see His dazzling glory. The Virgin's

words can be understood to mean that the special privilege granted to three disciples on Mount Thabor was being extended to the Medjugorje visionaries, and through them, to all who open their hearts to God.

10 All of the monthly messages beginning with January 1987 until publication are listed in the index, with the exception of those contained in the chapters.

11 Collette Webster, who was killed by a sniper in Mostar, did not come to Medjugorje as a pilgrim, but to work specifically as a volunteer to assist the war victims.